# Privacy and Security
# for Mobile Crowdsourcing

# RIVER PUBLISHERS SERIES IN DIGITAL SECURITY AND FORENSICS

*Series Editors:*

**ANAND R. PRASAD**
*Deloitte Tohmatsu Cyber LLC, Japan*

**R. CHANDRAMOULI**
*Stevens Institute of Technology, USA*

**ABDERRAHIM BENSLIMANE**
*University of Avignon, France*

**PETER LANGENDÖRFER**
*IHP, Germany*

The "River Publishers Series in Security and Digital Forensics" is a series of comprehensive academic and professional books which focus on the theory and applications of Cyber Security, including Data Security, Mobile and Network Security, Cryptography and Digital Forensics. Topics in Prevention and Threat Management are also included in the scope of the book series, as are general business Standards in this domain.

Books published in the series include research monographs, edited volumes, handbooks and textbooks. The books provide professionals, researchers, educators, and advanced students in the field with an invaluable insight into the latest research and developments.

Topics covered in the series include-

- Blockchain for secure transactions
- Cryptography
- Cyber Security
- Data and App Security
- Digital Forensics
- Hardware Security
- IoT Security
- Mobile Security
- Network Security
- Privacy
- Software Security
- Standardization
- Threat Management

For a list of other books in this series, visit www.riverpublishers.com

# Privacy and Security
# for Mobile Crowdsourcing

Shabnam Sodagari

**River Publishers**

Routledge
Taylor & Francis Group

NEW YORK AND LONDON

**Published 2023 by River Publishers**
River Publishers
Alsbjergvej 10, 9260 Gistrup, Denmark
www.riverpublishers.com

**Distributed exclusively by Routledge**
605 Third Avenue, New York, NY 10017, USA
4 Park Square, Milton Park, Abingdon, Oxon OX14 4RN

*Privacy and Security for Mobile Crowdsourcing* / by Shabnam Sodagari.

Routledge is an imprint of the Taylor & Francis Group, an informa business

ISBN 978-87-7022-861-9 (hardback)
ISBN 978-87-7004-059-4 (paperback)
ISBN 978-10-0381-141-1 (online)
ISBN 978-10-3263-084-7 (master ebook)

While every effort is made to provide dependable information, the publisher, authors, and editors cannot be held responsible for any errors or omissions.

# Contents

# Preface

Mobile crowdsourcing has driven numerous novel technological applications, including but not limited to online road status updates, city guides, software testing, journalism, connecting businesses with users, and several other imaginable operations. This book puts forward current knowledge for safeguarding crowdsensing participants including mobile workers, task requestors, and the server, with a focus on principles, tools, and design techniques. The learning objectives in each chapter progress gradually across the cognitive realm. The only prerequisite knowledge for Chapters 2 and 3 of this book is a basic understanding of probability. Readers lacking mathematical skills can still benefit from Chapters 1 and 4–11 of the book (essentially on applications and implication of technologies) and may skip Chapters 2 and 3. The book can be used by academic and industry professionals, researchers, engineers, scientists, and students. Each chapter is accompanied by the related bibliography for further reference. Additionally, the book contains several questions/answers and worked examples to clarify and emphasize essential principles. This book presents broad vantage points on how security and privacy methods operate for mobile crowdsourcing. Most importantly, the goal is to encourage exciting future applications.

Shabnam Sodagari

# List of Figures

# List of Tables

# List of Abbreviations

| | |
|---|---|
| BGV | Brakerski-Gentry-Vaikuntanathan |
| BLS | Boneh-Lynn-Shacham |
| CA | Certificate authority |
| CLS | Certificateless signature |
| CSP | Cellular service provider |
| D2D | Device to device (communication) |
| DDoS | Distributed denial of service |
| DGK | Damgård-Geisler-Krøigaard |
| DoS | Denial of service |
| DSS | Dynamic spectrum sharing |
| EM | Expectation maximization |
| FLP | Fischer-Lynch-Paterson |
| IIoT | Industrial internet of things |
| IMEI | International mobile equipment identity |
| IoV | Internet of vehicles |
| MCS | Mobile crowdsourcing/crowdsensing |
| NLP | Natural language processing |
| NLTCS | National long-term case study |
| pdf | Probability density function |
| PK | Public key |
| PKI | Public key infrastructure |
| PoS | Proof of stake |
| PoT | Proof of trust |
| PoW | Proof-of-work |
| QoE | Quality of experience |
| RFID | Radio frequency identification |
| RSS | Received signal strength |
| RSU | Road side unit |

| | |
|---|---|
| SHE | Somewhat homomorphic encryption |
| SINR | Signal to interference plus noise ratio |
| SSID | Service set identifier |
| UE | User equipment |
| VCG | Vickrey–Clarke–Groves |

# Introduction

Mobile crowdsourcing is a groundbreaking and vibrant ecosystem that facilitates the outsourcing of tasks to the wisdom of the crowd, as well as the expansion of resources that would otherwise be inaccessible. MCS systems owe their ever-increasing ubiquity to social networks, the Internet of Things (IoT), remote health, widespread mobile apps, and other factors. Nevertheless, MCS systems still need to be protected to prevent detrimental consequences of the exposure of personal information. The book discusses crowdsourcing and crowdsensing security and privacy models. Chapter 1 begins with an overview of the principles of crowdsourcing systems, their value, their applications, and the issues associated with the vulnerabilities of such systems. Chapter 2 explains spatio-temporal privacy techniques for mobile crowdsensing. Chapter 3 characterizes differential privacy techniques for obfuscation and crowdsourced data mining. Chapter 4 covers security of fog- and edge-based crowdsensing IoT. Blockchains to safeguard crowdsensing are treated in Chapter 5. The focus of Chapter 6 is on incentive mechanisms and game-theory methods to shield crowdsourcing. Machine learning security solutions for crowdsensed data aggregation are covered in Chapter 7. Crowdsourced mobile apps, reliability in crowdsensed industrial IoT, and crowdsourcing to mitigate misinformation and fake news are topics of Chapters 8–10. Security in 6G and Wi-Fi communication hotspots that leverage crowdsensing is discussed in Chapter 11. Representative problems are presented in Chapter 12.

The goal of the book is to provide insights into mainstay principles for protection of mobile crowdsourcing/crowdsensing systems, which are embodied by present and future use cases.

# 1

# The Importance of Crowdsourcing

After reading this chapter, you should be able to:

- List main components of mobile crowdsourcing infrastructure.
- Explain major applications of mobile crowdsourcing.
- Identify security and privacy risks in mobile crowdsourcing.
- Specify performance tradeoffs to benchmark the security and efficiency of mobile crowdsensing.

## 1.1 What is Crowdsourcing/Crowdsensing?

Crowdsourcing = crowd + outsourcing involves sourcing tasks to a group or a crowd rather than only an individual. The crowd may be composed of devices, Internet of Things (IoT) sensors, mobile phones, tablets, smart wearables, etc. Without loss of generality, we use the terms crowdsourcing and crowdsensing interchangeably in this book. The meaning will be clear from the context. Crowdsensing systems collect large data volumes through colossal sensing by widespread smartphone users, cyber–physical systems, social media, vehicles, human intelligence, etc., to solve complex tasks. The premise of mobile crowdsourcing/crowdsensing (MCS) is to tap into the power of crowd for performing tasks. Tasks can be performed by computing devices or humans.

QUESTION: What are some examples of MCS tasks?
ANSWER: MCS tasks span a large spectrum, including testing software, finding bugs, constructing databases or repositories, finding cures to illnesses, searching for missing people, learning about side effects of medications, word processing and proofreading, etc.

In our connected time, it is the right moment to study crowdsourcing or crowdsensing, due to the prolific number of mobile devices (e.g., smart phones), Internet connectivity, and the spread of IoT. Mobile crowdsourcing is enabled by the ubiquity of built-in sensors in mobile devices, such as cameras, microphones, accelerometers, GPS, etc.

QUESTION: What are the challenges associated with crowdsensing?

ANSWER: Some example challenges for the implementation of MCS include mechanisms to motivate the crowd to participate; mechanisms for obtaining data; minimizing errors; assessing the quality of performed tasks; allocating tasks to suitable participants; finding expert participants, etc.

QUESTIONS: What are some mechanisms to motivate participation in crowdsourcing?

ANSWER: Example motivations include financial income, having fun, working for altruistic and humanitarian causes, etc.

### 1.1.1 Economic market and value of crowdsourcing/crowdsensing

MCS is an economical solution to circumvent the need for large core networks, especially in time-sensitive services. Different economic sectors benefit from crowdsourcing, e.g., outsourced insurance claims processing. Crowdsourcing can even contribute to labor efficiency and mental health by asking users to report sensed noise pollution (loud music, noisy vehicles, construction noise, etc.) tagged with their locations to construct urban noise maps. Patients' data collected by wearable devices are sent to remote medical servers. MCS has already grown into a billion dollar market. For example, Waze was reported to be acquired by Google for $1.3 billion. The market value of crowd-testing alone (not to mention other numerous MCS platforms) is predicted, according to Bloomberg, to reach $3.16 billion by 2030.

Figure 1.1 demonstrates some examples of crowdsourcing marketplaces.[1] From tracking pandemics to applications, such as Google Maps, Uber, environmental monitoring, journalism, healthcare, crisis/disaster response, air quality control, noise and traffic monitoring, urban planning, etc., mobile crowdsourcing systems are interweaved with the society and daily lives. MCS finds applications in smart cities, pandemic monitoring, environment monitoring, healthcare, industrial IoT, smart homes, wearable devices, smart

---

[1]Figure 1.1 is not an exhaustive list of crowdsourcing platforms and many other examples can be found.

**Figure 1.1** Some examples of crowdsourcing platforms. These platforms range from carpooling, to city guides, wireless signal monitoring, weather monitoring, software testing, and numerous other use cases.

furniture, internet of vehicles, etc. For example, human computation can be leveraged for cleaning data (ProPublica). Interactive sharing of street information, such as accidents, as well as editing roads, landmarks, and local fuel prices are realized by crowdsensing. Ridesharing services and marketing surveys to guide decision making, etc., are only a few examples of commercial MCS platforms.

## 1.1.2 The structure of MCS systems

An MCS central server (trusted third-party) is the medium between requestors and workers to recruit workers to collect data for requestors. In other words, the server publishes spatio-temporal tasks of requesters to mobile workers, and mobile workers upload the collected data to the server once they complete the published tasks. For example, a requestor may need images of a particular scene. Mobile workers, who are closer to the scene, take pictures with their devices and send them to the requestor. Workers have some degree of freedom to select their spatio-temporal tasks according to their resources, social interests, schedule, etc. Rewards managed by MCS server incentivize mobile workers to provide requestors with desired quality of experience (QoE).

### 1.1.3 Security and privacy risks affecting MCS

Although crowdsourced data produce rich societal knowledge, they also cause unprecedented privacy and security threats to participants. For example, single point of failure is a threat to the centralized MCS architecture. Moreover, the data and private information are prone to malicious task requestors/workers or servers (internal threat), and hackers (external threat). Security and privacy vulnerabilities can cause detrimental financial, emotional, and psychological damages to the citizens of smart cities. The resulting consumer mistrust may hinder social innovation, which degrades social welfare and motivation, thereby imposing social cost. Therefore, it is of utmost importance for the aggregated crowdsourced data not to expose sensitive information, such as daily routines, personal health records, visited locations, political views, etc.

### 1.1.3.1 Untrustworthy MCS participants

Some types of security and privacy threats in mobile crowdsourcing systems can emerge from malicious or untrusted participants. Major attacks of this type are:

- identity or reputation forging by some workers;
- gaining undesired access to data;
- publishing a task by a requestor without a reward;
- task requestor curiosity about the private information of MCS workers, during their communication;
- conflicting behavior attack; and
- collusion attack.

In the conflicting behavior attack, malicious participants provide partially correct and partially false information to mislead the crowdsourcing system. In the collusion attack, malicious users collude to provide completely false information. False reporting, free riding, and data non-trustworthiness are among the threats in large-scale MCS networks. More specifically, false reporting means the task requester pays the worker after the execution of the task and lies about the quality of the work done by the MCS worker to reduce the payment of the worker. On the other hand, free riding involves a case when the task requester pays the worker before the execution of the task, but the worker does not complete the task.

### 1.1.3.2 Unreliable MCS server

Many crowdsourced systems rely on a trusted server with access to raw (non-obfuscated) data. However, the privacy of the worker or the requestor goes at risk when the MCS server cannot be trusted (internal attack), or when the MCS server is vulnerable to cyber-attacks and hacking, especially in real-time crowdsourcing. In such cases, the server should neither gain access to raw private data of participants nor use them for data aggregation. Instead, differential privacy mechanisms can be used before publishing the aggregated data (Chapter 3).

To distinguish a qualified user for a certain task, the MCS server may take advantage of users' context and history, such as location, time, profile, and activity in both offline and online task selection crowdsourced systems.

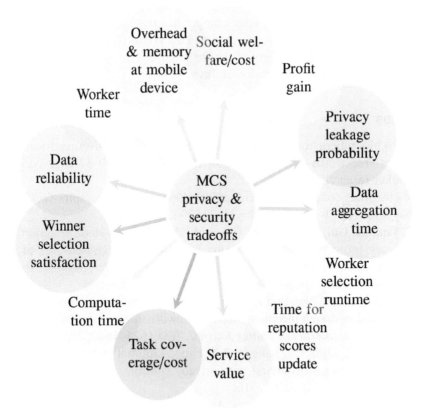

**Figure 1.2**   Performance tradeoffs and metrics for MCS security and privacy.

Nevertheless, disclosure of participant's data can jeopardize their privacy. For example, the spatio-temporal data of MCS participants can be disclosed by having sensing data on mobile devices being tagged with personal information. The revealed spatio-temporal private information can cause leakage of identity, personal activities, political views, health status, etc.

Figure 1.2 outlines some performance tradeoffs and metrics for MCS security and privacy. Some of the metrics in Figure 1.2 have negative correlations with others, i.e., enhancing one metric may degrade another. Therefore, it is critical to strike a balance among various parameters, depending on the crowdsensing application. Moreover, protection of workers' privacy is not only to the benefit of workers, but also to the benefit of requestors since it incentivizes the workers to accomplish the tasks. The coming chapters include major security and privacy challenges in MCS systems along with solutions and approaches, based on spatio-temporal privacy, $k$-anonymity, differential privacy, blockchains, edge-computing, machine learning, truth discovery, recommendation systems, games, etc. These techniques are the guiding principles for the design of future solutions to safeguard MCS systems against various types of vulnerabilities.

## References

https://www.bloomberg.com/press-releases/2022-07-14/crowdsourced-testi ng-market-size-worth-3-16-billion-globally-by-2030-at-9-37-cagr-veri fied-market-research.

https://www.forbes.com/sites/petercohan/2013/06/09/google-to-spite-faceb ook-buy-waze-for-1-3-billion/?sh=348335796228.

J. An, H. Yang, X. Gui, W. Zhang, R. Gui, and J. Kang. Tcns: Node selection with privacy protection in crowdsensing based on twice consensuses of blockchain. *IEEE Transactions on Network and Service Management*, 16 (3):1255–1267, 2019.

W. Chen, Y. Chen, X. Chen, and Z. Zheng. Toward secure data sharing for the iov: A quality-driven incentive mechanism with on-chain and off-chain guarantees. *IEEE Internet of Things Journal*, 7(3):1625–1640, 2020.

Y. Gong, L. Wei, Y. Guo, C. Zhang, and Y. Fang. Optimal task recommendation for mobile crowdsourcing with privacy control. *IEEE Internet of Things Journal*, 3(5):745–756, 2016.

J. Hu, H. Lin, X. Guo, and J. Yang. Dtcs: An integrated strategy for enhancing data trustworthiness in mobile crowdsourcing. *IEEE Internet of Things Journal*, 5(6):4663–4671, 2018.

J. Hu, K. Yang, K. Wang, and K. Zhang. A blockchain-based reward mechanism for mobile crowdsensing. *IEEE Transactions on Computational Social Systems*, 7(1):178–191, 2020.

C. Lai, M. Zhang, J. Cao, and D. Zheng. SPIR: A secure and privacy-preserving incentive scheme for reliable real-time map updates. *IEEE Internet of Things Journal*, 7(1):416–428, 2020.

T. Li, T. Jung, Z. Qiu, H. Li, L. Cao, and Y. Wang. Scalable privacy-preserving participant selection for mobile crowdsensing systems: Participant grouping and secure group bidding. *IEEE Transactions on Network Science and Engineering*, 7(2):855–868, 2020. doi: 10.1109/TNSE.2018.2791948.

W. Liu, X. Wang, and W. Peng. Secure remote multi-factor authentication scheme based on chaotic map zero-knowledge proof for crowdsourcing internet of things. *IEEE Access*, 8:8754–8767, 2020. doi: 10.1109/ACCESS.2019.2962912.

L. Ma, X. Liu, Q. Pei, and Y. Xiang. Privacy-preserving reputation management for edge computing enhanced mobile crowdsensing. *IEEE Transactions on Services Computing*, 12(5):786–799, 2019.

X. Ren, C. Yu, W. Yu, S. Yang, X. Yang, J. A. McCann, and P. S. Yu. LoPub : High-dimensional crowdsourced data publication with local differential privacy. *IEEE Transactions on Information Forensics and Security*, 13(9): 2151–2166, 2018.

Yuichi Sei and Akihiko Ohsuga. Differential private data collection and analysis based on randomized multiple dummies for untrusted mobile crowdsensing. *IEEE Transactions on Information Forensics and Security*, 12(4):926–939, 2017. doi: 10.1109/TIFS.2016.2632069.

Y. Wang, Y. Li, Z. Chi, and X. Tong. The truthful evolution and incentive for large-scale mobile crowd sensing networks. *IEEE Access*, 6:51187–51199, 2018. doi: 10.1109/ACCESS.2018.2869665.

Z. Wang, J. Hu, R. Lv, J. Wei, Q. Wang, D. Yang, and H. Qi. Personalized privacy-preserving task allocation for mobile crowdsensing. *IEEE Transactions on Mobile Computing*, 18(6):1330–1341, 2019a. doi: 10.1109/TMC.2018.2861393. ©[2019] IEEE. Reprinted, with permission.

Z. Wang, X. Pang, Y. Chen, H. Shao, Q. Wang, L. Wu, H. Chen, and H. Qi. Privacy-preserving crowd-sourced statistical data publishing with an untrusted server. *IEEE Transactions on Mobile Computing*, 18(6): 1356–1367, 2019b.

Y. Wu, S. Tang, B. Zhao, and Z. Peng. Bptm: Blockchain-based privacy-preserving task matching in crowdsourcing. *IEEE Access*, 7:45605–45617, 2019.

Qichao Xu, Zhou Su, Shui Yu, and Ying Wang. Trust based incentive scheme to allocate big data tasks with mobile social cloud. *IEEE Transactions on Big Data*, 8(1):113–124, 2022. doi: 10.1109/TBDATA.2017.2764925.

Y. Zhang, M. Li, D. Yang, J. Tang, G. Xue, and J. Xu. Tradeoff between location quality and privacy in crowdsensing: An optimization perspective. *IEEE Internet of Things Journal*, 7(4):3535–3544, 2020. doi: 10.1109/JIOT.2020.2972555.

S. Zou, J. Xi, H. Wang, and G. Xu. Crowdblps: A blockchain-based location-privacy-preserving mobile crowdsensing system. *IEEE Transactions on Industrial Informatics*, 16(6):4206–4218, 2020.

# 2

# Spatio-temporal Privacy of Crowdsourced Applications

After reading this chapter, you should be able to:

- Examine the main components of spatio-temporal privacy and $k$-anonymity in MCS systems.
- Explain privacy models for crowdsourced search.
- Analyze elements of secure crowdsensed object search.
- Assess the performance of privacy-preserving crowdsensed object search.

Table 2.1 contains the notation and variables frequently used in this chapter.

Crowdsourced data, such as road monitoring, indoor floor plan reconstruction, and smart transportation are tagged with locations. Even sensing data can be linked to users' locations. Location information may be disclosed during task allocation (untrusted server). Lack of location privacy may lead to physical surveillance, stalking, identity theft, breach of sensitive information (e.g., health status, political and religious views, etc.). Hence, disclosing true locations to the MCS server may be harmful to mobile workers.

## 2.1 Privacy-preserving Object Search by the Crowd

In this chapter, we consider the problem of finding a lost object through crowdsensing. Let us imagine that you forgot your belonging in an area, e.g., an airport. A unique Bluetooth tag is attached to your valuable object, which is now lost. As the owner of the object, you become a task requestor. Through your tablet, smartphone, or some other smart device, you submit a task to the MCS server to find your object. The MCS server broadcasts the task to mobile workers. Each mobile worker searches its vicinity for the lost

**Table 2.1**  Notation.

| | |
|---|---|
| ID | Bluetooth tag or radio frequency identity of an object |
| $\widetilde{\text{ID}}$ | ID of the lost object |
| PK | Task requestor's public key |
| $r$ | Random seed |
| $H$ | Hash function |
| $f$ | Number of timeslots in a frame |
| $K$ | Total number of hash functions |
| $q$ | Probability for a mobile worker to act as a dummy tag |
| $S$ | A two-dimensional geographic area |
| $W$ | Total number of mobile workers in area $S$ |
| $R$ | Radius of a circular area |
| $\varsigma$ | A subarea, i.e., $\varsigma \subsetneq S$ |
| $N(\varsigma)$ | Random variable representing the number of mobile workers in the subarea $\varsigma$ |
| $n$ | Realization of the random variable $N$ |
| $\mathbb{P}(l)$ | Probability mass function for a discrete random variable $l$ |
| $\mu$ | Average (expected value) of a discrete random variable |
| $P_{\text{FA}}$ | False alarm probability |

object. The mobile workers send their results to the MCS server. The MCS server forwards the results collected from workers to your tablet (the task requestor), which infers the location of the lost object based on the responses from mobile workers.

We are trying to answer the following questions:

- How can the task requestor hide the location of the lost objects from mobile workers who search for it? In other words, how can the mechanism ensure that only the object owner can discover the location of the lost object, and not the mobile workers, who search for the object?
- Is it possible to protect the location privacy of mobile workers against the task requestor?

Let us consider Figure 2.1. The lost object has a unique ID denoted by $\widetilde{ID}$ and the owner knows the approximate region where it was lost, e.g., the airport. Besides direct communication with Bluetooth or RFID object tags,

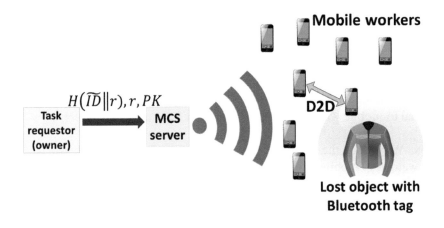

**Figure 2.1** Task requestor initiates a request to MCS server to find the lost object (e.g., a smart wearable) which has a Bluetooth tag attached to it.

mobile workers can communicate to each other via device to device (D2D) mechanisms, such as Wi-Fi direct, frequency hopping, etc. To initialize the crowdsourced search process:

- The task requestor sends its public key PK to the MCS server. Task requestor also sends a random seed $r$ and $H(\widetilde{ID}\|r)$. The latter denotes the result of a hash function taking as input a combination of $\widetilde{ID}$ and the random seed $r$. The hash function $H$ is publicly known.

> **What is a hash function?**
>
> A hash function takes variable length inputs and produces fixed-length outputs (also called digest).
> A hash function should not be reversible. It means one cannot guess what the input was to the hash function by looking at the hash digest.
> No two different inputs should have the same hash digest.

- After receiving the above three parameters, the MCS server forwards them to mobile workers in the area.
- Mobile workers broadcast the three-tuple $H(\widetilde{ID}\|r), r, \mathrm{PK}$ to their vicinity.

- The objects with Bluetooth tags receiving these parameters calculate the hash digest using their ID and the received random seed $r$, i.e., $H(ID\|r)$. They compare the result of their own $H(ID\|r)$ with the received hash digest $H(\widetilde{ID}\|r)$. Since the ID of the lost object is unique ($\widetilde{ID}$), the results match for the lost object. As such, the lost object can verify that this signal is intended for it. However, the lost object does not yet send any signal to mobile workers to hide its location from mobile workers.

QUESTION: Why does the task requestor send its public key, which is forwarded to mobile workers by the MCS server?

ANSWER: Since the task requestor wants to hide the results from MCS server, mobile workers use the public key to encrypt their findings before forwarding them to the MCS server. As such, only the task requestor can decipher the collected results.

QUESTION: Is there a way to ensure that the MCS server does not replace the public key of the task requestor with its own public key?

ANSWER: The task requestor (object owner) can replace the public key PK with a public-key certificate.

QUESTION: In the initialization phase, described above (Figure 2.1), the lost object hides its location by not immediately responding to mobile detectors and postponing the response to the next round. How does the task requestor (owner) find the location of the lost object?

ANSWER: In the next round of the algorithm (Figure 2.2), the task requestor sends a new random seed $r_1$ along with the number of timeslots $f$ in a frame to the MCS server. The MCS server broadcasts these two parameters to mobile workers. The mobile workers broadcast $r_1$ and $f$ to their area of coverage.

The lost object with unique $\widetilde{ID}$ and any other Bluetooth tag $i$ (with a unique $ID_i$) that receive $r_1$ and $f$ calculate $K$ hash functions using a combination of the tag's ID and $r_1$, i.e., $h_\kappa(ID\|r_1)$, $\kappa = 1, \ldots, K$ and $ID \in \{ID_i, \widetilde{ID}\}$. Each Bluetooth tag including the lost object responds in timeslots $h_\kappa(ID\|r_1)$ mod $f$.

The time slots in the frame are numbered $0, 1, \ldots, f - 1$. For example, in Figure 2.3, the result of $h_\kappa(ID\|r_1)$ mod $f$ coincides with time slot number $f - 3$. In general, for $\kappa = 1, \ldots, K$ and $ID \in \{ID_i, \widetilde{ID}\}$, the output of every $h_\kappa(\widetilde{ID}\|r_1)$ mod $f$ is a uniformly distributed random variable from 0 to $f - 1$ with probability $\frac{1}{f}$.

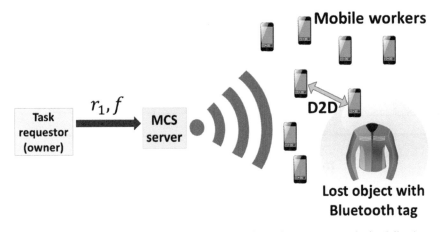

**Figure 2.2**  After task initialization in Figure 2.1, the task requestor sends the following to the MCS server: a new random seed $r_1$ and the number of timeslots $f$ in a frame. The MCS server broadcasts these two parameters to mobile workers.

To conceal the existence and location of the lost object from mobile workers, once a mobile worker locally broadcasts the random number and $f$, every other mobile worker in the target area hearing from another mobile worker chooses itself as a dummy tag with probability $q$. Mobile workers, which act as dummy tags send dummy responses (1 bit) in time slots obtained by $h_\kappa(ID_i\|r_1) \mod f$. Mobile workers near the lost object cannot differentiate between the responses from the lost object and dummy tag responses, since it is not only the lost object that sends responses. The mobile workers acting as dummy tags use a random pseudonym ID to calculate their response time slots instead of their real ID. If the task requestor and the MCS server do not collude, this allows no task requestor to link the location of mobile workers to their real IDs.

QUESTION: What if the MCS server and the task requestor collude? How can mobile workers preserve their location privacy?

ANSWER: In the absence of a trusted MCS server, mobile workers could use differential privacy for their locations. Differential privacy will be discussed in the next chapter.

Each time slot in Figure 2.3 can be either empty from any response or have one response from a tag, or include multiple responses resulting from

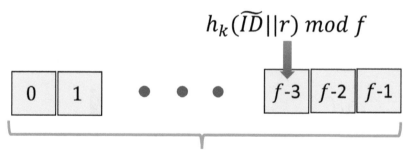

$$h_k(\widetilde{ID}\|r) \bmod f$$

**Frame of $f$ time slots**

**Figure 2.3** The response of either the lost object Bluetooth tag $(\widetilde{ID})$ or a dummy tag $(ID_i)$ is a bit "one" in the time slot number that results from $h_\kappa(ID\|r_1) \bmod f$ for $\kappa = 1, \ldots, K$ and $ID \in \{ID_i, \widetilde{ID}\}$.

coinciding of the outputs of

$$h_\kappa(ID\|r_1) \quad \bmod f \tag{2.1}$$
$$\kappa = 1, \ldots, K$$
$$ID \in \{ID_i, \widetilde{ID}\}.$$

The coincidence of $h_\kappa(ID\|r_1) \bmod f$ can be from either multiple hash functions for the same tag (including the lost object) or from multiple objects with Bluetooth tags (different IDs). We assume that there is a method for resolving collision for overlaid responses that occur in the same time slots.

The responses are collected by mobile workers. At the end of each round, each mobile worker sends a vector of bits containing the responses it received to the MCS server to be sent to the task requestor.

QUESTION: How does the task requestor determine which mobile workers are closer to the lost object and which ones are not?

ANSWER: The task requestor checks each mobile worker's bit vector. Specifically, the task requestor checks all time slots related to $h_\kappa(\widetilde{ID}\|r_1) \bmod f$ for all $\kappa = 1, \ldots, K$. These time slots represent the responses of the lost object. Mobile workers whose collected report does not contain all of these time slots (they report a 0 bit in either slots of the lost object $h_\kappa(\widetilde{ID}\|r_1) \bmod f$ for $\kappa = 1, \ldots, K$) are excluded by the task requestor, since the lost object is not in their vicinity. The task requestor does not announce which mobile workers are excluded from the search. Otherwise, mobile workers and the server will know which mobile workers are near the lost object, which eventually leads them to localize the lost object. The task requestor keeps a list of mobile workers whose report included all time slots resulting from $h_\kappa(\widetilde{ID}\|r_1) \mod f$, where $\kappa = 1, \ldots, K$. The lost object may be close to this latter group of mobile workers, but it could also be due to a false alarm, caused by coincidence of dummy responses.

QUESTION: How does the task requestor verify if the remaining list of mobile workers are really close to the lost object or if it was only a coincidence (caused by dummy tags) that caused their time slots to match those of the lost object?

ANSWER: The task requestor runs the next round by sending a new random seed $r_2$ to the MCS server. Once mobile workers receive this new random seed, they broadcast it to their area of coverage and the algorithm proceeds similar to the previous round to collect reports of time slot responses. The time slot responses are calculated using the new random seed $r_2$ for the hash function, i.e., $h_\kappa(\widetilde{ID}\|r_1) \mod f$, where $\kappa = 1, \ldots, K$ and $ID \in \{ID_i, \widetilde{ID}\}$.

QUESTION: How many dummy tags exist in the vicinity of one mobile worker?

ANSWER: In an area with $W$ other mobile workers, if each of them decides to act as a dummy tag with probability $q$, there will be almost $\lfloor qW \rfloor$ dummy tags around each mobile worker.

QUESTION: When is the search process finished?

ANSWER: When the task requestor cannot exclude more mobile workers. In other words, when in at least two consecutive rounds, the list of remaining mobile workers remains the same.

QUESTION: In the final round, the task requestor retrieves the locations of the remaining mobile workers from the MCS server. This may cause the MCS server to localize the lost object. Is it possible for the task requestor not to reveal to the MCS server which mobile workers are eliminated from the search?

ANSWER: Mobile workers encrypt their locations with the public key of the task requestor, which was sent to them upon initialization of the search (Figure 2.1). To prevent the MCS server to learn the location of the remaining mobile workers deemed close to the lost object, the task requestor can retrieve the encrypted locations of both the remaining mobile workers and some excluded mobile workers to confuse the MCS server. Another solution could be for the task requestor to use private information retrieval, which allows obtaining the encrypted locations of candidate mobile workers without revealing to the MCS server which locations were retrieved. As such, neither the service provider nor the remaining mobile workers know the location of the lost object.

## 2.2 How Accurate is the Crowdsensed Object Search?

As mentioned before, the output of every $h_\kappa(\widetilde{ID}\|r_1) \bmod f$ is a discrete random variable[1], uniformly distributed in $\{0, 1, \ldots, f - 1\}$ with probability $\frac{1}{f}$.

We previously discussed that even if the task requestor finds a bit vector (reported by a mobile worker) to exactly match the time slots that the lost object (with the unique ID) should have responded, it may be due to a coincidence of dummy tags' responses. In other words, the lost object is not close to any mobile worker, but some dummy tags happen to respond exactly in the same time slots as the lost object. This is called a false alarm. One reason that the search extends over the next rounds with new random seeds is to reduce false alarm probability.

QUESTION: Denote the total number of mobile workers by $W$ in a two-dimensional geographic area $S$. The average density of mobile workers in the unit area will be $\frac{W}{S}$. If the whole area $S$ has $W$ mobile workers on average, what is the **average** number of mobile workers in a circle with radius $R$?

ANSWER: There are in average $\lfloor \pi R^2 \frac{W}{S} \rfloor$ mobile workers in a circle with area $\pi R^2$.

QUESTION: What is the probability that there is no mobile worker in the vicinity of the lost object?

ANSWER: The previous question discussed the average number of mobile workers that could exist in a subarea of $S$. However, in general, the number of mobile workers in any subarea $\varsigma \subset S$ is a random variable. The Poisson point process for the distribution of mobile

---

[1]©[2016] IEEE. reprinted, with permission, from J. Sun *et al.*, "SecureFind: Secure and Privacy-Preserving Object Finding via Mobile Crowdsourcing," *IEEE Trans. on Wireless Communications*, vol. 15, no. 3, pp. 1716-1728, March 2016

workers (with mean $\frac{W}{S}$) in subarea $\varsigma \subset S$ is

$$\mathbb{P}[N(\varsigma) = n] = \left(\varsigma\frac{W}{S}\right)^n \exp\left(-\varsigma\frac{W}{S}\right)\frac{1}{n!}. \tag{2.2}$$

Denote by $R$ the coverage radius of signals for both the mobile workers and the Bluetooth tag of the lost object. Therefore, the coverage area of the lost object is a circle with area $\varsigma = \pi R^2$. The probability that there is no mobile worker in this subregion is obtained by setting $n = 0$ and $\varsigma = \pi R^2$ in the above spatial Poisson process. Note that $0! = 1$.

$$\mathbb{P}[N\left(\pi R^2\right) = 0] = \left(\pi R^2\frac{W}{S}\right)^0 \exp\left(-\pi R^2\frac{W}{S}\right)\frac{1}{0!} = \exp\left(-\pi R^2\frac{W}{S}\right). \tag{2.3}$$

## 2.2.1 False alarm

Now, consider the false alarm case, when the lost object is not in the coverage area of any mobile worker, but dummy tags' responses just happen to coincide with the same time slots of the lost object.

QUESTION: Using the Poisson spatial process for the distribution of mobile workers, how many dummy tags can be found near a mobile worker with a coverage radius of $R$?

ANSWER: We previously discussed that there are on average $\lfloor \pi R^2\frac{W}{S}\rfloor$ mobile workers in the circle of area $\pi R^2$. Each mobile worker acts as a dummy tag with probability $q$. Therefore, there are $\lfloor q\pi R^2\frac{W}{S}\rfloor$ other mobile workers that send dummy responses.

QUESTION: How many total dummy responses are sent in $f$ timeslots?

ANSWER: Since there are $K$ hash functions and there are $\lfloor q\pi R^2\frac{W}{S}\rfloor$ dummy tag transmitters, the total number of dummy responses are $K\lfloor q\pi R^2\frac{W}{S}\rfloor$.

QUESTION: What is the probability that no dummy responses land in a time slot that belongs to the lost object?

ANSWER: Let us consider one time slot in which the lost object sends its response. The probability that one dummy tag responds in this time slot is $\frac{1}{f}$ (uniform distribution of responses for $f$ timeslots). The complement of this probability means that this dummy tag does not respond in this certain time slot, which is $1 - \frac{1}{f}$. However, this result is only for one dummy tag and one hash function. There are a total of $Kq\lfloor \pi R^2 \frac{W}{S} \rfloor$ dummy responses. Therefore, the probability that no dummy responses coincide with a time slot that belongs to the lost object is

$$\underbrace{\left(1 - \frac{1}{f}\right) \cdots \left(1 - \frac{1}{f}\right)}_{K\lfloor q\pi R^2 \frac{W}{S} \rfloor} = \left(1 - \frac{1}{f}\right)^{K\lfloor q\pi R^2 \frac{W}{S} \rfloor}. \tag{2.4}$$

QUESTION: How many distinct time slots are possible for the response of the lost object?

ANSWER: This is similar to the problem of $f$ bins (time slots in a frame) and $K$ balls (outputs of $K$ hash functions mod $f$). Two example extreme possible combinations include: The $K$ balls thrown all in one bin (one distinct time slot at minimum) or each ball thrown in its distinct bin ($K$ distinct time slots at maximum). All other distinct time slots ranging from 1 to $K$ are possible (Figure 2.4). When $l$ out of $K$ balls fall in distinct bins (time slots), it means that $K - l$ of them fall in the same bins (time slots). Noting that the probability of a response of the lost object in each time slot is $\frac{1}{f}$, the probability

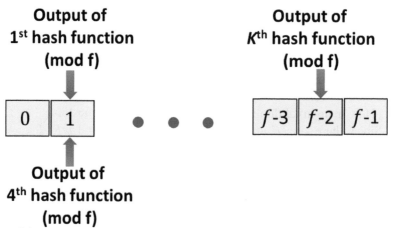

**Figure 2.4** An example of possible distinct time slots. In this particular example, without loss of generality, the outputs of the first and the fourth hash functions modulo $f$ happen to be in the same time slot. To calculate the possible number of distinct time slots, note the similarity with the problem of throwing $K$ balls (outputs of $K$ hash functions modulo $f$) into $f$ bins (time slots).

for the response of the lost object to appear in $l$ distinct time slots is

$$\binom{f}{l}\frac{1}{f^l}\frac{1}{f^{(K-l)}} = \binom{f}{l}\frac{1}{f^K}. \tag{2.5}$$

QUESTION: Using the above probability for $l$ distinct time slots in the response of the lost object, find the **average** number of distinct time slots in the response of the lost object.

ANSWER: The average of a discrete random variable $l$ with probability mass function $\mathbb{P}(l)$ is defined as

$$\sum_{\forall l} l\,\mathbb{P}(l). \tag{2.6}$$

Insert $\binom{f}{l}\left(\frac{1}{f}\right)^K$ for $\mathbb{P}(l)$ and note that $l$ takes on values from 1 to $K$. The response of the lost object appears on average in the following number of distinct time slots:

$$\mu = \sum_{\forall l} l\,\mathbb{P}(l) = \sum_{l=1}^{K} l\binom{f}{l}(\frac{1}{f})^K. \tag{2.7}$$

QUESTION: What is the probability that in a single round of the crowdsensed search, a dummy tag responds in exactly all of the $\mu$ distinct slots that on average belong to the lost object?

ANSWER: Recall that the probability that no dummy responses coincide with the time slot of the lost object was previously derived to be

$$\left(1 - \frac{1}{f}\right)^{K\lfloor q\pi R^2 \frac{W}{S}\rfloor}. \tag{2.8}$$

The probability that a dummy response and the lost object response coincide for one time slot is the complement of the above probability, i.e.,

$$1 - \left(1 - \frac{1}{f}\right)^{K\lfloor q\pi R^2 \frac{W}{S}\rfloor}. \tag{2.9}$$

In order for all $\mu$ time slots of the lost object to overlap with a dummy response, the previous event must happen for $\mu$ time slots, with the following probability:

$$\varphi = \left(1 - \left(1 - \frac{1}{f}\right)^{K\lfloor q\pi R^2 \frac{W}{S}\rfloor}\right)^{\mu}. \tag{2.10}$$

Following the above analysis, we are now ready to calculate the probability of the false alarm. Recall that the task requestor continues the rounds of crowdsensed search until the list of mobile workers that cannot be excluded from the search does not change for at least two consecutive rounds. For a search that takes a total of $T$ rounds, false alarm happens when the dummy response time slots coincide exactly with all the time slots of the response of the lost object for all $T$ rounds. The probability that one dummy tag survives all $T$ rounds and remains in the list of the task requestor is $\varphi^T$. Therefore, the probability that this single dummy tag does not survive the list in all $T$ rounds is $1 - \varphi^T$. However, there are $K\lfloor q\pi R^2 \frac{W}{S} \rfloor$ of those dummy tags. Thus, the probability that none of them survive the list for all the $T$ rounds is

$$\left(1 - \varphi^T\right)^{K\lfloor q\pi R^2 \frac{W}{S} \rfloor}. \tag{2.11}$$

False alarm chance is the complement of the above probability, i.e., **at least** one dummy tag survives the list of candidates for the task requestor in all the rounds of the search, since its time slot responses exactly coincided with that of the lost object. Therefore, the false alarm probability is

$$P_{\text{FA}} = 1 - \left(1 - \varphi^T\right)^{K\lfloor q\pi R^2 \frac{W}{S} \rfloor}. \tag{2.12}$$

## 2.3 *k*-Anonymity Cloaking for MCS Privacy

Sensitive attributes of published tasks on the crowdsourcing platform may be used by malicious workers that link them to other public databases to reveal private information of requestors. $k$-anonymity is a spatio-temporal cloaking method for privacy protection, especially when the spatio-temporal information of MCS participants need to be tagged to the collected data.

$k$-anonymity may be combined with differential privacy to achieve location privacy in location-based crowdsourcing. One example application is New York City's CityNoise app in which people submit the sensed noise pollution data tagged with locations to generate urban noise maps. $k$-anonymity may degrade the accuracy of task performance by causing information loss. The tradeoff between $k$-anonymity privacy and service quality degradation can be modeled by Stackelberg games or by optimization formulations. For example, one can maximize the number of protected users, subject to a location quality degradation constraint or simply minimize the MCS task

**Table 2.2** Solutions for *k*-anonymity cloaking for MCS privacy.

| Goal | Approach | Evaluation |
|---|---|---|
| Tradeoff between *k*-anonymity and accuracy | Probability-based matrix to estimate the lower and upper bounds of the crowdsourcing accuracy for the anonymized data; feedback-based *k*-anonymity by synthetic samples published to human workers; adaptively cutting the dimensions based on feedback results on the synthetic samples | Applied on Mondrian algorithm and evaluated on U.S. census dataset |
| Location privacy in location-based MCS services while maintaining the quality of service | • Combining *k*-anonymity, differential privacy, and Stackelberg game to solve the tradeoff between privacy and service quality<br>• Optimization formulations | Benchmarked with Clique cloaking and differential perturbation |

quality degradation, while guaranteeing the location privacy for all users. Furthermore, probability models for the tradeoff between privacy and accuracy in *k*-anonymity can give probabilistic lower and upper bounds for task accuracy. Searching for the optimal anonymity approach is a NP-hard problem, which needs to be solved by heuristics. Progressive feedback histogram by repeatedly submitting the crowdsourced tasks to collect the humans' opinions and then adaptively adjusting the anonymity approach may enhance the accuracy in the anonymization process.

## 2.3.1 Integration of *k*-anonymity with incentive mechanisms

Once MCS users are clustered into groups for *k*-anonymity, reverse auction incentives may be applied to mitigate the information loss. As such, users are recruited based on group values, compensations, and sensing costs for clustered groups. Since *k*-anonymity (e.g., in location aggregation) implies approximate values, the algorithm approximation ratio is a determining factor in the reverse auction design. Table 2.2 highlights *k*-anonymity applications in MCS spatio-temporal privacy.

## 2.3.2 Future research directions

Some research directions on applying *k*-anonymity in MCS include: studying the effects of social relationships among MCS workers on *k*-anonymity;

extensions to personalized *k*-anonymity models, where each user requires a different anonymity level; and *k*-anonymity models tailored for crowdsensing that perturb spatio-temporal information for time-sensitive crowdsensed data.

## References

Z. Chi, Y. Wang, Y. Huang, and X. Tong.  The novel location privacy-preserving ckd for mobile crowdsourcing systems.  *IEEE Access*, 6: 5678–5687, 2018. doi: 10.1109/ACCESS.2017.2783322.

P. Huang, X. Zhang, L. Guo, and M. Li.  Incentivizing crowdsensing-based noise monitoring with differentially-private locations.  *IEEE Transactions on Mobile Computing*, 20(2):519–532, 2021.  doi: 10.1109/TMC.2019.2946800.

Jingchao Sun, Rui Zhang, Xiaocong Jin, and Yanchao Zhang.  Securefind: Secure and privacy-preserving object finding via mobile crowdsourcing. *IEEE Transactions on Wireless Communications*, 15(3):1716–1728, 2016. doi: 10.1109/TWC.2015.2495291.  ©[2016] IEEE. reprinted, with permission.

X. Wang, Z. Liu, X. Tian, X. Gan, Y. Guan, and X. Wang.  Incentivizing crowdsensing with location-privacy preserving.  *IEEE Transactions on Wireless Communications*, 16(10):6940–6952, 2017.  doi: 10.1109/TWC.2017.2734758.

Y. Wang, Y. Li, Z. Chi, and X. Tong. The truthful evolution and incentive for large-scale mobile crowd sensing networks. *IEEE Access*, 6:51187–51199, 2018. doi: 10.1109/ACCESS.2018.2869665.

S. Wu, X. Wang, S. Wang, Z. Zhang, and A. K. H. Tung.  K-anonymity for crowdsourcing database. *IEEE Transactions on Knowledge and Data Engineering*, 26(9):2207–2221, 2014. doi: 10.1109/TKDE.2013.93.

Y. Zhang, M. Li, D. Yang, J. Tang, G. Xue, and J. Xu.  Tradeoff between location quality and privacy in crowdsensing: An optimization perspective.  *IEEE Internet of Things Journal*, 7(4):3535–3544, 2020.  doi: 10.1109/JIOT.2020.2972555.

# 3

# Differentially Private Mobile Crowdsourcing

After reading this chapter, you should be able to:

- Recognize the elements of differentially private MCS design.
- Integrate differential privacy with data mining MCS systems.
- Apply differential privacy to MCS systems operating on a distance metric.
- Evaluate task allocation in differentially private MCS.

This chapter examines the use of differential privacy for geo-obfuscation for MCS workers. Table 3.1 contains the notation and variables frequently used in this chapter.

## 3.1 Differentially Private Location Obfuscation of MCS Participants

Location-privacy incentivizes the crowd to report sensed data. Consider a location-based MCS, in which task allocation is based on the distances between tasks and mobile workers. In the presence of an untrusted server, location disclosure may not be to the benefit of mobile workers. Such a case is more worrying for mobile workers who are not allocated any task, since their locations are disclosed without earning any payment. Differential privacy is particularly useful for the location privacy of MCS participants in the presence of an untrusted server by removing the need for any trusted third-party.

**Example:** Consider two databases $x$ and $x'$ containing grades of a number of students. We say that the two databases are adjacent, when they only differ in one person. An outside observer makes a query to the databases to obtain a property $Z$. The property $Z$ could be asking for the average grade without

**Table 3.1**   Notation.

| | |
|---|---|
| $x, x'$ | Two databases or two different location topologies for a mobile worker |
| $\zeta(w_i, t_j)$ | Equals 1 if the MCS server allocates worker $w_i$ to task $t_j$ and equals 0 otherwise |
| $\Gamma_i$ | Random variable denoting Laplace noise for the $i$th mobile worker $w_i$ |
| $\gamma_i$ | Realization of the Laplacian noise random variable $\Gamma_i$ |
| $Z$ | Output property observed as a result of a query |
| $F_x(Z)$ | Probability that database (or location topology) $x$ outputs $Z$ as a result of a query |
| $\rho_j$ | Publishing radius of task $t_j$ |
| $d_{ij}$ | Distance between the $i$th mobile worker and the $j$th task |
| $\widetilde{d_{ij}}$ | Obfuscated distance between the $i$th mobile worker and the $j$th task |
| $\mathbb{P}[\ ]$ | Probability of an event |
| $\epsilon_i$ | Privacy leakage level of $i$th mobile worker |
| $M$ | Number of tasks that $i$th mobile worker is interested in |
| $\mathbb{R}^M$ | $M$-tuple representing the set of actual distances of the $i$th mobile worker to its $M$ tasks of interest |

knowing the grade of each individual. For example, the query returns the property $Z$ to be:

- 85% as the average grade from database $x$ (containing five students);
- 90% as the average grade from database $x'$ (containing four students).

Let $g_1, \ldots, g_5$ denote the grades of students $1, \ldots, 5$.

$$\frac{g_1 + \cdots + g_4 + g_5}{5} = 85\% \tag{3.1}$$
$$\frac{g_1 + \cdots + g_4}{4} = 90\%.$$

By solving the above equations, the outside observer easily obtains the grade $g_5$, causing the privacy of the databases to be lost.

The above example shows that we need a mechanism for indistinguishability in order to preserve privacy. Indistinguishability is at the core of differential privacy.

---

### What is Differential Privacy?

An obfuscation mechanism $F$ is $\varepsilon$-differential private if for any two adjacent databases $x$ and $x'$, and any property (output) $Z$, the probability distributions $F_x$ and $F_{x'}$ differ on $Z$ at most by $\exp(\varepsilon)$. By notation:

$$F_x(Z) \leq \exp(\varepsilon)F_{x'}(Z). \tag{3.2}$$

$F_x(Z)$ relates to the probability that in response to a query, database $x$ outputs a property belonging to the set $Z$. Likewise, $F_{x'}(Z)$ relates to the probability that database $x'$ outputs the same queried property, i.e., an output belonging to the set $Z$. Even if the adversary knows the obfuscation mechanism $F$, the adversary cannot distinguish between the actual individual secret values.

---

On one side, knowledge of the precise locations of MCS participants helps the centralized server with the optimal task allocation to minimize MCS workers' travel distances to the task location. On the other side, MCS workers risk their location privacy when uploading sensed data tagged with their actual positions, especially in sparse MCS systems.

QUESTION: In a personalized differentially private approach, each mobile worker uploads the personal privacy leakage to the MCS server along with obfuscated distances to tasks. How can the MCS server determine which mobile worker should be allocated to perform the task despite obfuscated information?

ANSWER: When MCS workers use obfuscated information, the worker selection mechanism for task allocation becomes probabilistic to minimize the cost of the total travel distance. As such, each task is allocated to the worker who has the largest probability of being closest to it.

After the worker selection, selected workers are paid based on their travel cost and desired privacy leakage level. The payment mechanism needs to satisfy truthfulness, profitability, and probabilistic individual rationality, which will be discussed later in this chapter.

If $x$ and $x'$ are locations instead of databases, we can adapt differential privacy toward location privacy. At the core of this notion is probabilistic geo-obfuscation for geographic locations to replace the actual locations. This leads to differential privacy for distances.

---

**Differential Privacy using Distance Metric**

For any two locations $x$ and $x'$, if the distance between these two locations, i.e., $\mathscr{D}(x, x') \leq \rho$, the difference between the distributions $F_x$ and $F_{x'}$ should be at most $\epsilon\rho$. This can be obtained by letting $\varepsilon = \epsilon\rho$ in eqn. (3.2), i.e.,

$$F_x(Z) \leq \exp(\epsilon\rho)F_{x'}(Z), \tag{3.3}$$

$\epsilon$ can be interpreted as the level of privacy leakage at one unit of distance. A smaller value for $\epsilon$ implies more privacy.

---

Note that $\rho$ is an upper bound for the distance $\mathscr{D}(x, x')$. Instead of the upper bound of the distance, we can directly insert the distance into eqn. (3.2) by letting $\varepsilon = \epsilon\mathscr{D}(x, x')$ to obtain

$$F_x(Z) \leq \exp(\epsilon\mathscr{D}(x, x'))F_{x'}(Z). \tag{3.4}$$

Consider MCS applications that collect spatio-temporal data, e.g., for creating city guides in urban areas. When MCS server allocates tasks to workers based on their distances to the tasks, it still suffices for system operations, if mobile workers report their distances to the tasks and not their actual locations. This is a step toward workers' location privacy; since the MCS server will only know that the mobile worker is on the boundary of a circle (around the task) with the reported travel distance radius, but will not know its actual location. However, even in this case, if the MCS server has prior knowledge about the distribution and frequency of visiting places for a worker, worker's location may not be fully private. Therefore, it is inevitable for workers to obfuscate their distances to the tasks before reporting them to the MCS server. To this end, workers can use the Laplace mechanism that will be explained in this chapter.

The $j$th task is denoted by $t_j$. The travel distance between task $t_j$ and mobile worker $w_i$ is $\mathscr{D}(w_i, t_j)$ or $d_{ij}$ for short, as in Figure 3.1.

In addition to dealing with obfuscated distances to determine task allocation and worker payments, the MCS server has to minimize costs by minimizing aggregate travel distances for all tasks. To minimize travel distances, a publishing radius can be considered around each task[1]. Only mobile

---

[1] ©[2019] IEEE. Reprinted, with permission, from Z. Wang *et al.*, "Personalized Privacy-Preserving Task Allocation for Mobile Crowdsensing," *IEEE Transactions on Mobile Computing*, vol. 18, no. 6, pp. 1330-1341, 1 June 2019

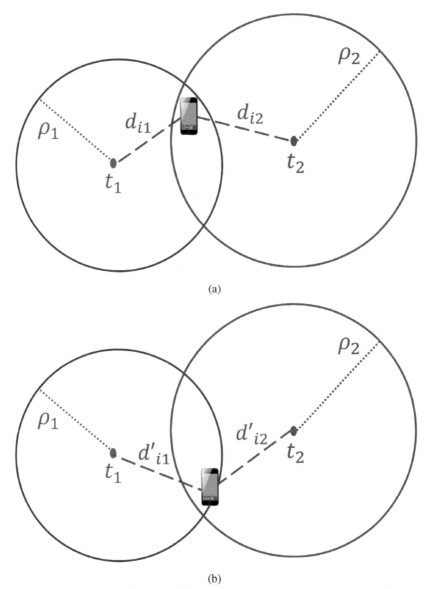

(a)

(b)

**Figure 3.1**   Ideally, a mobile worker *i* does not want the MCS server to distinguish between the two topologies (a) and (b) related to the location of the mobile worker. Location-based tasks $t_1$ and $t_2$ are at the centers of circles with radii $\rho_1$ and $\rho_2$, respectively. The reason for MCS server to publish and allocate a task within its specific radius is to limit the maximum travel distance, thereby putting a cap on the payment.

workers located inside the publishing circle of a task can receive the task or apply for it. The publishing region of task $t_j$ is a circle with radius $\rho_j$.

In Figure 3.1, the publishing radius of tasks $t_1$ and $t_2$ are $\rho_1$ and $\rho_2$, respectively. In topology (a), the distances of mobile worker $i$ to tasks $t_1$ and $t_2$ are $d_{i1}$ and $d_{i2}$, respectively. In topology (b), the distances of mobile worker $i$ to the same tasks are $d'_{i1}$ and $d'_{i2}$, respectively. The goal is to design a task allocation strategy and evaluate its accuracy, not to allow the MCS server to locate mobile worker $i$. This is achieved by preventing the MCS server from being able to distinguish topology (a) from topology (b) in Figure 3.1.

QUESTION: Can you establish an analogy between topologies (a) and (b) in Figure 3.1 and eqn. (3.2)?
ANSWER: Topologies (a) and (b) are analogous to $x$ and $x'$ in eqn. (3.2) and this has led us to eqn. (3.3).

For instance, the travel distance metric $d_{ij}$ can be the absolute value of the differences of the locations of worker $w_i$ and task $t_j$, defined as $d_{ij} = \mathscr{D}\left(w_i, t_j\right) = |l_{w_i} - l_{t_j}|$. Here, $l_{w_i}$ and $l_{t_j}$ are the locations of worker $w_i$ and task $t_j$, respectively.

QUESTION: Do you know of a probability density function that shows similarity with the absolute value distance metric as defined above?
ANSWER: The absolute value distance metric shows similarity with the deja vu Laplacian probability density function. Therefore, intuitively, one method to achieve differential privacy is the Laplace mechanism.

---

### Laplace Mechanism

The Laplace mechanism takes a value that needs to be protected as the input and outputs the input plus noise. The noise random variable is derived from a Laplacian distribution. Formally, the reported value $z \in Z$ is obtained by adding Laplace noise to input $x$. For mobile worker $i$, Laplace noise is a random variable $\Gamma_i$ with zero mean ($\mathbb{E}[\Gamma_i] = 0$) derived from a Laplacian probability density function (pdf), i.e.,

$$\Gamma_i \sim \frac{\epsilon_i}{2} \exp\left(-\epsilon_i |\gamma_i|\right) \tag{3.5}$$

where $\epsilon_i$ is a parameter of the Laplacian pdf and $\gamma_i$ is a realization of the random variable $\Gamma_i$.

The obfuscated distance $\widetilde{d_{ij}}$ between worker $w_i$ and task $t_j$ is obtained by adding Laplace noise to the actual distance $d_{ij}$. The Laplace mechanism is applied to locations as follows:

$$d_{ij} + \gamma_i = \widetilde{d_{ij}}. \tag{3.6}$$

Note that $d_{ij}$ is only known to worker $i$. When a realization $\gamma_i$ of the zero-mean Laplace noise $\Gamma_i$ is added to $d_{ij}$, the resulting obfuscated distance $\widetilde{d_{ij}}$ will be a Laplace random variable centered around the mean $(d_{ij})$ with the same variance as $\Gamma_i$. We can insert $\gamma_i = \widetilde{d_{ij}} - d_{ij}$ from eqn. (3.6) into eqn. (3.5):

$$\frac{\epsilon_i}{2} \exp\left(-\epsilon_i |\widetilde{d_{ij}} - d_{ij}|\right). \tag{3.7}$$

Note that $|\widetilde{d_{ij}} - d_{ij}|$ is a distance metric for the differences of the two distances $\widetilde{d_{ij}}$ and $d_{ij}$.

Let us consider how the MCS server performs probabilistic task allocation for a task $t_k$. Several mobile workers may apply and compete for task $t_k$ by sending their privacy leakage levels and their obfuscated distances. The MCS server has to answer the following question: What is the closest worker to the task, given the uploaded obfuscated distances and personal privacy leakage levels? The answer lies in finding the worker with the largest probability of being closest to the task.

For instance, two mobile workers $w_i$ and $w_g$ apply to a task $t_j$. Mobile worker $w_i$ uploads $\epsilon_i$ and $\widetilde{d_{ij}}$ to the MCS server.

$$\widetilde{d_{ij}} = d_{ij} + \gamma_i \tag{3.8}$$

where $\gamma_i$ is a realization of the Laplacian random variable

$$\Gamma_i \sim \frac{\epsilon_i}{2} \exp\left(-\epsilon_i |\gamma_i|\right).$$

Similarly, mobile worker $w_g$ uploads $\epsilon_g$ and $\widetilde{d_{gj}}$.

$$\widetilde{d_{gj}} = d_{gj} + \gamma_g \tag{3.9}$$

where $\gamma_g$ is a realization of the Laplacian random variable

$$\Gamma_g \sim \frac{\epsilon_g}{2} \exp\left(-\epsilon_g |\gamma_g|\right).$$

The MCS server finds

$$\mathbb{P}[d_{ij} \leq d_{gj}] = \mathbb{P}[\widetilde{d}_{ij} - \gamma_i \leq \widetilde{d}_{gj} - \gamma_g] = \mathbb{P}[\widetilde{d}_{ij} - \widetilde{d}_{gj} \leq \gamma_i - \gamma_g] = \quad (3.10)$$

$$\int \int_{\gamma_i - \gamma_g \geq \widetilde{d}_{ij} - \widetilde{d}_{gj}} f\left(\gamma_i, \gamma_g\right) d\gamma_i d\gamma_g.$$

Here, $f\left(\gamma_i, \gamma_g\right)$ is the joint pdf (probability density function) of two Laplace noise random variables $\Gamma_i$ and $\Gamma_g$. The double integral is taken over a region for which $\gamma_i - \gamma_g \geq \widetilde{d}_{ij} - \widetilde{d}_{gj}$.

Since the noises for different mobile workers are independent

$$f\left(\gamma_i, \gamma_g\right) = f\left(\gamma_i\right) f\left(\gamma_g\right). \quad (3.11)$$

For independent Laplace noise variables $\gamma_i$ and $\gamma_g$, the joint pdf is

$$f\left(\gamma_i\right) f\left(\gamma_g\right) = \frac{\epsilon_i}{2} \exp\left(-\epsilon_i |\gamma_i|\right) \frac{\epsilon_g}{2} \exp\left(-\epsilon_g |\gamma_g|\right) = \frac{\epsilon_i \epsilon_g}{4} \exp\left(-\epsilon_i |\gamma_i| - \epsilon_g |\gamma_g|\right). \quad (3.12)$$

Therefore, eqn. (3.10) becomes

$$\int \int_{\gamma_i - \gamma_g \geq \widetilde{d}_{ij} - \widetilde{d}_{gj}} f\left(\gamma_i, \gamma_g\right) d\gamma_i d\gamma_g = \quad (3.13)$$

$$\int \int_{\gamma_i - \gamma_g \geq \widetilde{d}_{ij} - \widetilde{d}_{gj}} f\left(\gamma_i\right) f\left(\gamma_g\right) d\gamma_i d\gamma_g = \quad (3.14)$$

$$\int_{-\infty}^{\infty} \int_{-\infty}^{\gamma_i - \left(\widetilde{d}_{ij} - \widetilde{d}_{gj}\right)} f\left(\gamma_i\right) f\left(\gamma_g\right) d\gamma_g d\gamma_i. \quad (3.15)$$

QUESTION:  In the above analysis, what criterion do you suggest the MCS server to use for the selection of a worker for the task?

ANSWER: If $\mathbb{P}[d_{ij} \leq d_{gj}] \geq 50\%$, then worker $w_i$ is selected for the $j$th task $(t_j)$.

QUESTION: The payment of the MCS server to the selected mobile worker is composed of two parts that are linearly proportional to 1) travel distance and 2) privacy level. In other words, the travel distance of the mobile worker to the allocated task is used by the MCS server to determine part of the payment (besides the payment incentive for loosening the privacy). Can a mobile worker $i$ gain more payment by being non-truthful about reported travel distance $\widetilde{d}_{ij}$?

ANSWER: If the payment for travel distance to a mobile worker $i$ (selected to perform the task) is directly proportional to the reported $\widetilde{d}_{ij}$, a mobile worker can gain more payment by reporting a larger obfuscated travel distance. A non-truthful mobile worker can do so by adding Laplace noise to an augmented $\check{d}_{ij} \geq d_{ij}$, instead of the true $d_{ij}$.

QUESTION: What is a payment mechanism to implement truthfulness among mobile workers?

ANSWER: If the MCS server pays the selected mobile worker proportional to the travel distance reported by the second bidding mobile worker, then no mobile worker will have incentives to augment their reported travel distance. This is similar to the Vickrey auction, where a bidder offering the highest bid is selected, but the payment is equal to the second bid value.

QUESTION: How does the above payment strategy, based upon the second smallest travel distance reported by workers (instead of the smallest travel distance reported by the selected worker), prevent non-truthful travel distance reporting?

ANSWER: If the augmented falsified uploaded travel distance happens to exceed at least one other travel distance of some other worker, the cheating mobile worker does not get the task (and any payment). If the augmented falsified travel distance is still the lowest among all other mobile workers, the cheating mobile worker $i$ gets task $t_j$. However, the non-truthful worker cannot increase its payment, because either way, the payment is based on the second smallest travel distance bid among all workers. It means that no mobile worker will be better off by being non-truthful. Nevertheless, if the mobile workers collude, the above-mentioned payment mechanism cannot implement truthfulness.

We next analyze the differential privacy of the discussed mechanism.

Let $X_i \in \mathbb{R}^M$ be an $M$-tuple for the set of actual distances of worker $w_i$ to its $M$ tasks of interest. Likewise, $X'_i \in \mathbb{R}^M$ is another $M$-tuple representing the set of actual distances of worker $w_i$ to its $M$ tasks of interest in another topology, where the locations of tasks do not change, but the location of the mobile worker changes.

$Z_i \in \mathbb{R}^M$ is the set of obfuscated reported distances of worker $w_i$ when this worker applies for its $M$ tasks of interest. More specifically, $Z_i = X_i + (\gamma_{i1}, \ldots, \gamma_{iM})$. The noise parameters $\gamma_{i1}, \ldots, \gamma_{iM}$ that worker $i$ adds to its distances to each of the $M$ tasks (of interest) are realizations of the following zero-mean Laplace random variables, respectively:

$$\Gamma_{i1} \sim \frac{\epsilon_{i1}}{2} \exp\left(-\epsilon_{i1}|\gamma_{i1}|\right) \tag{3.16}$$

$$\vdots$$

$$\Gamma_{iM} \sim \frac{\epsilon_{iM}}{2} \exp\left(-\epsilon_{iM}|\gamma_{iM}|\right).$$

Since the noise random variables $\Gamma_{i1}, \ldots, \Gamma_{iM}$ are generated by a single mobile worker $(w_i)$, we can assume that they are identically distributed, i.e.,

$$\epsilon_{i1} = \cdots = \epsilon_{iM} = \epsilon_i.$$

**Example:** In Figure 3.1(a) with $M = 2$ tasks of interest for mobile worker $i$, we have

$$X_i = (d_{i1}, d_{i2}) \tag{3.17}$$

$$Z_i = \left(\widetilde{d_{i1}}, \widetilde{d_{i2}}\right) = (d_{i1} + \gamma_1, d_{i2} + \gamma_2). \tag{3.18}$$

Define the probability that topology $X_i$ outputs a property $Z_i$ as $\mathbb{P}_{X_i}[Z_i]$. Then,

$$\mathbb{P}_{X_i}[Z_i] = \mathbb{P}[\left(\widetilde{d_{i1}}, \widetilde{d_{i2}}\right)] = \mathbb{P}[\gamma_1 = \widetilde{d_{i1}} - d_{i1}, \gamma_2 = \widetilde{d_{i2}} - d_{i2}] \tag{3.19}$$

$$\overset{(a)}{=} \mathbb{P}[\gamma_1 = \widetilde{d_{i1}} - d_{i1}]\mathbb{P}[\gamma_2 = \widetilde{d_{i2}} - d_{i2}] \tag{3.20}$$

$$\overset{(b)}{=} \frac{\epsilon_i}{2} \exp\left(-\epsilon_i|\widetilde{d_{i1}} - d_{i1}|\right) \frac{\epsilon_i}{2} \exp\left(-\epsilon_i|\widetilde{d_{i2}} - d_{i2}|\right) \tag{3.21}$$

$$= \left(\frac{\epsilon_i}{2}\right)^2 \exp\left(-\epsilon_i\left(|\widetilde{d_{i1}} - d_{i1}| + |\widetilde{d_{i2}} - d_{i2}|\right)\right). \tag{3.22}$$

Equality $(a)$ follows by the independence of noise random variables and $(b)$ results from identically distributed Laplace noise variables for one mobile worker.

We can write the same relations for Figure 3.1(b) (a different location topology for the $i$th mobile worker) by letting

$$X_i' = \left(d_{i1}', d_{i2}'\right) \tag{3.23}$$

$$Z_i = \left(\widetilde{d_{i1}}, \widetilde{d_{i2}}\right) = \left(d_{i1}' + \gamma_1', d_{i2}' + \gamma_2'\right). \tag{3.24}$$

Then, the probability that the different topology $X_i'$ outputs the same queried property $Z_i$ is

$$\mathbb{P}_{X_i'}[Z_i] = \mathbb{P}[\gamma_1' = \widetilde{d_{i1}} - d_{i1}', \gamma_2' = \widetilde{d_{i2}} - d_{i2}']. \tag{3.25}$$

The goal is to examine the upper bound of differential privacy achieved by the Laplace mechanism for the two topologies. Differential privacy is determined by the ratio of probabilities of observing the same property $Z_i$ for two different topologies $X_i$ and $X'_i$. We extend the example of two tasks of interest (Figure 3.1) to any number $M$ of tasks.

QUESTION: Referring to Figure 3.1, what is the upper bound for $|d_{ij} - d'_{ij}|$?

ANSWER: The definition of publishing radius $\rho_j$ implies that the distance of the mobile worker to each task must be less than the publishing radius (for a mobile worker to be considered for a task). Therefore, $0 \leq d_{ij} \leq \rho_j$ and $0 \leq d'_{ij} \leq \rho_j$. The maximum difference $|d_{ij} - d'_{ij}|$ is obtained when $d_{ij} = \rho_j$ and $d'_{ij} = 0$ or vice versa. Hence, $\rho_j$ is an upper bound for the difference, i.e., $0 \leq |d_{ij} - d'_{ij}| \leq \rho_j$. We will use this result in the analysis of differential privacy.

QUESTION: Show that the Laplace mechanism for worker $w_i$ with $M$ tasks of interest meets $\epsilon_i \sum_{j=1}^{M} \rho_j$-privacy.

ANSWER: Writing the ratio of probability distributions yields

$$\frac{\mathbb{P}_{X_i}[Z_i]}{\mathbb{P}_{X'_i}[Z_i]} = \frac{\mathbb{P}_{X_i}[\widetilde{d_{i1}}, \ldots, \widetilde{d_{iM}}]}{\mathbb{P}_{X'_i}[\widetilde{d_{i1}}, \ldots, \widetilde{d_{iM}}]} \tag{3.26}$$

$$\overset{(a)}{=} \frac{\mathbb{P}[\gamma_1 = \widetilde{d_{i1}} - d_{i1}, \ldots, \gamma_M = \widetilde{d_{iM}} - d_{iM}]}{\mathbb{P}[\gamma'_1 = \widetilde{d_{i1}} - d'_{i1}, \ldots, \gamma'_M = \widetilde{d_{iM}} - d'_{iM}]}$$

$$\overset{(b)}{=} \frac{\mathbb{P}[\gamma_1 = \widetilde{d_{i1}} - d_{i1}], \ldots, \mathbb{P}[\gamma_M = \widetilde{d_{iM}} - d_{iM}]}{\mathbb{P}[\gamma'_1 = \widetilde{d_{i1}} - d'_{i1}], \ldots, \mathbb{P}[\gamma'_M = \widetilde{d_{iM}} - d'_{iM}]}$$

$$\overset{(c)}{=} \frac{\frac{\epsilon_i}{2} \exp\left(-\epsilon_i |\widetilde{d_{i1}} - d_{i1}|\right) \ldots \frac{\epsilon_i}{2} \exp\left(-\epsilon_i |\widetilde{d_{iM}} - d_{iM}|\right)}{\frac{\epsilon_i}{2} \exp\left(-\epsilon_i |\widetilde{d_{i1}} - d'_{i1}|\right) \ldots \frac{\epsilon_i}{2} \exp\left(-\epsilon_i |\widetilde{d_{iM}} - d'_{iM}|\right)}$$

$$\overset{(d)}{=} \prod_{j=1}^{M} \frac{\exp\left(-\epsilon_i |\widetilde{d_{ij}} - d_{ij}|\right)}{\exp\left(-\epsilon_i |\widetilde{d_{ij}} - d'_{ij}|\right)}$$

$$= \prod_{j=1}^{M} \exp\left(\epsilon_i \left(|\widetilde{d_{ij}} - d'_{ij}| - |\widetilde{d_{ij}} - d_{ij}|\right)\right)$$

$$\overset{(e)}{\leq} \prod_{j=1}^{M} \exp\left(\epsilon_i |d_{ij} - d'_{ij}|\right) \quad \text{by triangle inequality}$$

$$= \exp\left(\epsilon_i \left(\sum_{j=1}^{M} |d_{ij} - d'_{ij}|\right)\right) \overset{(f)}{=} \exp\left(\epsilon_i \|X_i - X'_i\|_1\right).$$

Equality $(a)$ follows from eqns. (3.8) and (3.24). Equality $(b)$ results from the assumption of independent noise variables. Equalities $(c)$ and $(d)$ follow from the Laplace pdf and canceling common terms from the numerator and denominator, respectively. $(e)$ is a result of triangle inequality, while equality $(f)$ is obtained from the definition of $L_1$ norm meaning that

$$\sum_{j=1}^{M} |d_{ij} - d'_{ij}| = \|X_i - X'_i\|_1.$$

As was shown before, when each task $t_j$ is associated with a geographic publishing region of radius $\rho_j$, then $|d_{ij} - d'_{ij}| \leq \rho_j$. As a result,

$$\sum_{j=1}^{M} |d_{ij} - d'_{ij}| = \|X_i - X'_i\|_1 \leq \sum_{j=1}^{M} \rho_j.$$

Therefore, for worker $w_i$ with privacy leakage level $\epsilon_i$, the Laplace mechanism satisfies $\epsilon_i \sum_{j=1}^{n} \rho_j$-privacy.

When mobile workers use the Laplace mechanism to obfuscate their distances to their tasks of interest, they are allowed to have different privacy leakage levels ($\epsilon$) from each other.

The mobile worker $w_i$ can apply for multiple tasks by sending $(t_j, \widetilde{d_{ij}})$ as well as its own privacy leakage $\epsilon_i$ to the MCS server. The MCS server decides about the task allocation. In other words, $\zeta(w_i, t_j) = 1$ denotes that the MCS server allocates task $t_j$ to mobile worker $w_i$; otherwise, $\zeta(w_i, t_j) = 0$.

Consider a case where a mobile worker can express interest in more than one task but will be allocated to a maximum of one task. The MCS server needs to solve the following integer linear program for optimal task allocation, facing the challenge of obfuscated distances instead of actual distances.

$$\min \sum_{\forall t_j} \sum_{\forall w_i} \zeta(w_i, t_j) d_{ij} \tag{3.27}$$

s. t. $\zeta\left(w_i, t_j\right) \in \{0, 1\}$ (3.28)

$$\sum_{\forall t_j} \zeta(w_i, t_j) \leq 1, \quad \forall i \qquad \text{No worker gets more than one task}$$

$$\sum_{\forall w_i} \zeta(w_i, t_j) = 1, \quad \forall j \qquad \text{No task is left unassigned}$$

The above optimization could be more precise if the actual distances $d_{ij}$ were known. However, only obfuscated distances $\widetilde{d_{ij}}$ are uploaded to the server (in addition to personal privacy leakage levels $\epsilon_i$).

Additionally, the MCS system needs to be truthful and satisfy individual rationality for both task requestors and mobile workers. Before defining the individual rationality for a mobile worker, we define the utility of a mobile worker. Utility $U_{ij}$ of worker $w_i$ who is selected for task $t_j$, i.e., $\zeta\left(w_i, t_j\right) = 1$, is the difference of the received payment $P_{ij}$ and the cost $C_{ij}$ that mobile worker $i$ has to bear to perform the allocated task, i.e.,

$$U_{ij} = P_{ij} - C_{ij}. \qquad (3.29)$$

The cost $C_{ij}$ that a mobile worker has to incur is composed of travel cost to the location of the allocated task and the privacy cost. The former (travel) cost is proportional to $d_{ij}$ and the latter (privacy) cost is proportional to the privacy leakage $\epsilon_i$ of worker $w_i$.

---

**Truthfulness**

A mechanism is truthful if no mobile worker can increase its utility by cheating about the parameters uploaded to the server, including the worker's travel distance and privacy leakage.

---

**Individual Rationality for Mobile Workers**

A mobile worker who is assigned to an MCS task needs to have a non-negative utility, i.e., $U_{ij} \geq 0$.

---

**Individual Rationality for Task Requestors**

The task requestor needs to benefit from the task. It means the value of each task should be at least as large as the amount paid to the mobile worker assigned to it.

QUESTION: Does a mobile worker $i$ have motivation to cheat about reporting their privacy leakage parameter $\epsilon_i$, when uploading it to the
MCS server?

ANSWER: The payment mechanism of the server incentivizes higher $\epsilon_i$ by
being directly proportional to the reported $\epsilon_i$. It means that mobile
workers who are willing to give up some of their privacy receive
more payment in exchange. Therefore, the utility of mobile workers
will not increase if they are not truthful about their desired privacy
leakage.

In other words, when a mobile worker chooses to loosen the privacy (larger $\epsilon_i$), the mobile worker receives more payment. This
is an incentive that the MCS server provides for mobile workers
to encourage them to report more accurate distances to the tasks
to enable the MCS server to more efficiently allocate the tasks to
workers.

The mobile worker $i$ uploads two parameters, i.e., $\epsilon_i$ and $\widetilde{d_{ij}}$ (obfuscated
distance using the addition of Laplace noise), to the MCS server. If the
obfuscation is done locally at mobile phones, a cheating mobile worker may
report a larger $\epsilon_i$, while actually deriving its noise from a Laplace distribution
with a lower $\epsilon_i$. By doing so, the cheating mobile worker can gain more
payment from the MCS server, while actually enjoying stricter privacy. In
this regard, a countermeasure against an untrusted mobile worker or MCS
server is to deploy multiple distributed agents to aggregate and perturb the
crowdsensed results (e.g., by adding Laplace perturbation) to ensure data
privacy. The agents then upload the results to the MCS server. This scheme
relies on the assumption that the server and distributed agents cannot collude
with each other. An MCS participant can randomly select an agent at each
time and upload its information to that agent through onion routing for
anonymous connection.

As was mentioned, differential privacy provides an upper bound on the
information obtained by third parties regardless of their prior knowledge.
Under the assumption of prior knowledge, distortion privacy ensures that
the expected inference error is larger than a threshold. When differentially
private geo-obfuscation is combined with distortion privacy, users obfuscate their reported locations under the guarantees of both differential and
distortion privacy. MCS workers can be partitioned based on worker density and non-uniform worker distribution. After the geo-obfuscation phase,
tasks are allocated based on geocast region selection methods that balance

workers' travel distances, system overhead, the number of workers that are notified of available tasks, and the success rate of task assignment. In general, task allocation may involve a mixed-integer non-linear optimization, which can be solved by the Benders decomposition and genetic algorithms. Since location obfuscation may degrade the task performance quality in MCS, an optimization solution needs to be devised to find the tradeoff between efficiency of assigning tasks and privacy of MCS users. For example, linear programming can learn the optimal location obfuscation function by fitting the original sensing data to the obfuscated location. The linear program constraints include differential-privacy, distortion-privacy, and evenly distributed obfuscation. MCS participants can determine the extent to which their information and context can be shared with the MCS server. Based on the shared information, the MCS server decides if the user should be recruited.

### 3.1.1 Differential privacy for data mining by statistical inference in crowdsourced data aggregation

Both differential privacy and cryptography fail to protect the aggregated statistics over crowdsourced data. For example, the true number of crowd-sourcing participants in an area can still be accurately exposed to an untrusted server. The two data types that need to be protected are as follows:

1. qualitative or categorical data (e.g., screen deployment);
2. quantitative data (e.g., location data, discrete meter readings, ordinal preference options, etc.).

Local differential privacy sanitizes each mobile user's data on the mobile device to preserve privacy when crowdsourced data is used for distribution estimation. For discrete distribution estimation from categorical crowdsourced data, a $k$-subset mechanism with mutual information metric is used, whereas for discrete quantitative data (with any distance metric, e.g., $L_2$ norm), an extension of $k$-subset mechanism, as a variant of the exponential mechanism, is used to tackle the asymmetry in data. Both these cases aim to minimize the mean distribution estimation error.

Randomized response, which involves sending the disguised value of a sensed category, preserves privacy even when the MCS server and all but one MCS participants collude. In randomized response-based MCS, each MCS participant generates a Bloom filter, using multiple hash functions to encode data into a unique bit string. Then, each bit is perturbed – before being sent to MCS server – according to the outcomes of a certain number of coin flips. For example, an MCS worker sends either the true data with probability $p$ or the disguised data with probability $1 - p$. The MCS server analyzes the statistics of crowdsensed data in lieu of precise information from sensing results. Randomized response anonymization can be extended to generate multiple disguised values (instead of one) from a single sensing result. The MCS server generates an estimated contingency or cross-tabulation table (multi-dimensional histogram) for distribution estimation. Under $\epsilon$-differential privacy constraint, the MCS server minimizes the expected values of utility metrics, such as mean squared error or Jensen–Shannon divergence that measures the difference between the contingency table and the estimated distribution.

Nonetheless, randomized response methods require a lot of samples to converge to an estimation. Another privacy-preserving method in data mining over crowdsourced data is the generation of a synthetic dataset with similar statistical distributions as the original crowdsourced data. To this end, marginal and multi-dimensional distributions are learned from the data after dimensionality and sparsity reduction. Particularly, expectation maximization and Lasso regression estimate the joint distributions and correlations among attributes, while MCS participants cloak their original data by applying randomized response on Bloom filter data records. Once the probability distribution is estimated from crowdsensed data, we have the following:

1. Correlated attributes are identified by measuring the mutual information and split into low-dimensional heterogeneous clusters to form an undirected dependency graph.
2. The attributes are split according to pruning the junction tree built from the dependency graph.
3. The low-dimensional datasets are sampled according to the connectivity of attribute clusters and the estimated distributions on each attribute cluster to synthesize an approximate dataset that replaces the original crowdsourced data to preserve privacy.

Table 3.2 summarizes differential privacy approaches for MCS.

## 3.1.2 Future research directions

Extension of the existing differentially private MCS models for homogeneous task values to heterogeneous crowdsourcing tasks; shortening the run-time of current methods; designing online schemes without the assumption of prior

**Table 3.2** MCS systems based on differential privacy.

| Goal | Approach | Evaluation metrics |
|---|---|---|
| MCS worker selection with differentially private worker location data | Probabilistic mechanism to minimize the travel distance by selecting workers with the largest probability of being closest to tasks; Vickrey payment mechanism by considering movement cost and privacy level | Truthfulness; profitability; probabilistic individual rationality |
| Maximizing differentially private MCS revenue under a limited budget, while achieving truthfulness | Multi-armed bandit dynamic pricing | Regret; revenue; privacy leakage; individual rationality |
| Privacy-preserving multi-dimensional joint distribution estimation for data mining from high-dimensional crowdsourced data | Finding correlations among multiple attributes to reduce the dimensionality of crowdsourced data; expectation maximization and Lasso regression for faster distribution estimation; randomized response applied to Bloom filter data features | Computation and communication overhead; data utility; estimation speed; accuracy benchmarked with support vector machines and random forest classification; mean square error and Jensen–Shannon divergence in crowdsensed data mining; mutual information and $L_2$-norm error evaluated on crowdsensed radiation levels in 23 Tokyo wards with 100,000 participants |
| Reducing the loss of MCS task performance due to obfuscated locations and inference attack without a trusted third party | Distortion privacy combined with differential privacy to bound the expected location inference error against inference attack; learning the function to fit the sensing data to obfuscated locations | Data quality loss; computation time; approximation ratio on traffic monitoring data |
| Original data feature preservation in differentially private randomized crowdsourced data collection | Supervised machine learning for predicting randomized data | Accuracy and true positives on MHEALTH dataset |

**Table 3.2**    *Continued.*

| Goal | Approach | Evaluation metrics |
|---|---|---|
| Leakage of prior knowledge to adversaries through correlation in crowdsourced data | Adding noise to aggregated data for differential privacy and applying randomized perturbation to remove data correlation | Privacy leakage evaluated on National Long-Term Case Study (NLTCS) dataset from StatLib, and search logs of Google Trends data |

knowledge about the number of users; continuous-pricing instead of discrete pricing; evaluation of the existing methods on other datasets; and extensions of differentially private location information to databases of trajectories of MCS participants' positions are among areas that need to be further explored.

## References

Konstantinos Chatzikokolakis, Miguel E. Andrés, Nicolás Emilio Bordenabe, and Catuscia Palamidessi. Broadening the scope of differential privacy using metrics. In Emiliano De Cristofaro and Matthew Wright, editors, *Privacy Enhancing Technologies*, pages 82–102, Berlin, Heidelberg, 2013. Springer Berlin Heidelberg.

Jianwei Chen, Huadong Ma, Dong Zhao, and Liang Liu. Correlated differential privacy protection for mobile crowdsensing. *IEEE Transactions on Big Data*, 7(4):784–795, 2021. doi: 10.1109/TBDATA.2017.2777862.

Y. Gong, L. Wei, Y. Guo, C. Zhang, and Y. Fang. Optimal task recommendation for mobile crowdsourcing with privacy control. *IEEE Internet of Things Journal*, 3(5):745–756, 2016.

K. Han, H. Liu, S. Tang, M. Xiao, and J. Luo. Differentially private mechanisms for budget limited mobile crowdsourcing. *IEEE Transactions on Mobile Computing*, 18(4):934–946, 2019. doi: 10.1109/TMC.2018.2848265.

X. Ren, C. Yu, W. Yu, S. Yang, X. Yang, J. A. McCann, and P. S. Yu. LoPub : High-dimensional crowdsourced data publication with local differential privacy. *IEEE Transactions on Information Forensics and Security*, 13(9): 2151–2166, 2018.

Yuichi Sei and Akihiko Ohsuga. Differential private data collection and analysis based on randomized multiple dummies for untrusted mobile crowdsensing. *IEEE Transactions on Information Forensics and Security*, 12(4):926–939, 2017. doi: 10.1109/TIFS.2016.2632069.

Y. Tsou and B. Lin. PPDCA: Privacy-preserving crowdsourcing data collection and analysis with randomized response. *IEEE Access*, 6: 76970–76983, 2018. doi: 10.1109/ACCESS.2018.2884511.

L. Wang, D. Zhang, D. Yang, B. Y. Lim, X. Han, and X. Ma. Sparse mobile crowdsensing with differential and distortion location privacy. *IEEE Transactions on Information Forensics and Security*, 15:2735–2749, 2020. doi: 10.1109/TIFS.2020.2975925.

L. Wang, D. Yang, X. Han, D. Zhang, and X. Ma. Mobile crowdsourcing task allocation with differential-and-distortion geo-obfuscation. *IEEE Transactions on Dependable and Secure Computing*, 18(2):967–981, 2021. doi: 10.1109/TDSC.2019.2912886.

S. Wang, L. Huang, Y. Nie, X. Zhang, P. Wang, H. Xu, and W. Yang. Local differential private data aggregation for discrete distribution estimation. *IEEE Transactions on Parallel and Distributed Systems*, 30(9):2046–2059, 2019a. doi: 10.1109/TPDS.2019.2899097.

Z. Wang, J. Hu, R. Lv, J. Wei, Q. Wang, D. Yang, and H. Qi. Personalized privacy-preserving task allocation for mobile crowdsensing. *IEEE Transactions on Mobile Computing*, 18(6):1330–1341, 2019b. doi: 10.1109/TMC.2018.2861393. ©[2019] IEEE. Reprinted, with permission.

Z. Wang, X. Pang, Y. Chen, H. Shao, Q. Wang, L. Wu, H. Chen, and H. Qi. Privacy-preserving crowd-sourced statistical data publishing with an untrusted server. *IEEE Transactions on Mobile Computing*, 18(6): 1356–1367, 2019c.

M. Yang, T. Zhu, Y. Xiang, and W. Zhou. Density-based location preservation for mobile crowdsensing with differential privacy. *IEEE Access*, 6:14779–14789, 2018. doi: 10.1109/ACCESS.2018.2816918.

# 4

# Trust in Edge- and Fog-based Vehicular Crowdsensing

After reading this chapter, you should be able to:

- List the main components of secure fog- and edge-based MCS.
- Explain the infrastructure of secure crowdsensed Internet of Vehicles (IoV).
- Construct defense mechanisms against sybil attacks on vehicular crowdsensing.

Edge/fog computing in MCS relieves the time delay and high bandwidth costs of centralized cloud computing by shifting the computational resources closer to the edge of the network, resulting in location awareness and mobility support. Since fog nodes are closer to the network edge than the cloud server, they can more accurately allocate MCS tasks to suitable workers. Fog-assisted confidential data deduplication eliminates extra communication overhead between fog nodes and the cloud. Moreover, blockchain-based solutions for integrity can be implemented in an edge computing environment.

Registration of participants by a trusted third party to receive the keys may alleviate external attacks on MCS systems, since external attackers have not received the keys. Even if external attackers intercept and replay messages of legitimate entities, they will not be able to pass the time-slot-based hash message. The stages of a privacy-preserving fog-assisted spatial crowdsensing are as follows:

1. Each task requestor anonymously (via a pseudonym) sends the encrypted task (using bilinear pairing and homomorphic encryption) and task requirements, such as aggregation types and obfuscated sensing area to the MCS server.
2. The MCS server assigns tasks to the fog nodes based on sensing area.

43

**Table 4.1**  Secure edge- and fog-assisted MCS.

| Goal | Approach | Evaluation metrics |
|------|----------|--------------------|
| Privacy-preserving and collusion-resistant aggregation of MCS workers' data and responding to requests with certificate authority | One-way hash chains, marked mix-nets, and grouping-based secure searchable encryption | Mutual information for privacy quantification; computational cost and communication overhead |
| Elimination of duplicate sensed data collected in MCS without exposing data content | BLS-oblivious pseudorandom function to enable fog nodes to detect and remove replicate data | Communication overhead |
| Privacy of MCS workers in task allocation (fog to workers) and confidentiality of task content in data aggregation | Bilinear pairing and homomorphic encryption by supporting statistics, such as sum, mean, variance, minimum, etc. | Computation/ encryption cost at each MCS participant |
| Differentially private real-time task allocation with the help of edge nodes | Binary tree noise aggregation to reduce the distortions induced by Laplace mechanism for differential privacy | Regret comparison with online learning algorithms; balance between privacy and accuracy |

3. Fog nodes decrypt the task and announce it to the local mobile workers.
4. A worker interested in a task requests the credentials of task authorization from the MCS server (e.g., task secrets).
5. After task completion, each worker hides the sensed data with a random number and encrypts data with its public key and sends it to fog nodes.
6. Fog nodes authenticate and verify the integrity of received encrypted data and compute the encrypted aggregation with the MCS server using the additive homomorphic property.
7. The MCS server attaches its digital signature to the encrypted result (integrity) and sends it to the task requestor who then decrypts it.

Table 4.1 provides an overview of the roles of fog nodes in private and secure MCS.

The MCS server should not be able to link the content and the identity of any task requestor. For privacy-preserving data aggregation, secure multi-party aggregation using statistics, such as sum, mean, variance, and minimum on encrypted data are adopted. Edge-enhanced context-aware task allocation enables real-time crowdsensing. The role of the cloud in task allocation may include evaluating the workers' reputations (based on background information, task context, historical feedbacks, rewards, etc.) and sending a subset of the most eligible workers to the edge. Then, the edge optimally allocates the tasks based on task requirements (such as maximizing the sensing coverage under a budget constraint) and workers' real-time information. Nevertheless, in the reputation update process, the privacy of both requesters and workers needs to be protected. The pool of MCS workers needs to be large enough, to allow for differential privacy to be effective.

Data encryption to protect sensing data may make it more challenging to calculate the reputation of malicious workers. As a countermeasure, the reputation value may be updated based on the deviations of the encrypted sensing data from the final collected truth. Nevertheless, this method reveals the exact deviation value of each worker to the reputation manager and may also expose the final collected truth through collusion with some MCS participants. Instead, the reputation may be updated by considering the rank of deviations.

Fog nodes can detect and remove replicate data (without accessing the content of crowdsensed data) using BLS-oblivious pseudo-random functions, thereby protecting the privacy of MCS workers. To hide identities of workers during data collection (anonymity), Chameleon hash function enables the MCS participants to anonymously claim their contributions for reward and identify greedy workers that want to receive their reward more than once. Fog nodes detect identical sensing data while not learning about the data itself by using BLS signature to generate the encryption key of sensing data. The key-homomorphic signature to sign the sensing data enables fog nodes to aggregate the signatures of MCS participants, to let the MCS server know about the contributions of the workers who generate replicate crowdsensed data.

The collusion scenarios in a fog-assisted MCS may include:

1. some workers and the cloud MCS server sharing their keys and collected crowdsourced data with each other;
2. collusion among workers and fog nodes;
3. requesters and cloud collusion;
4. requesters and fog nodes collusion.

Methods involving one-way hash chains, marked mix-nets, and grouping-based secure searchable encryption are used to thwart the above collusions as follows:

- The worker sends data containing a pseudo-identity, a multiencryption of the message, and a hash to the fog node.
- The fog node partially decrypts and shuffles the encrypted message to make ciphertexts unlinkable before sending to the cloud server.
- A task requester sends a request, containing a pseudo-identity, a group of encrypted indices, and a signature to a fog node.
- The fog node sends the received request to the cloud.

The next section discusses fog-assisted trustworthy vehicular MCS.

## 4.1 Trustworthy Vehicular MCS

An important element of smart transportation, autonomous vehicles, and vehicular social networks is the Internet of Vehicles (IoV). Some applications of vehicular crowdsensing include:

- road surface monitoring, location, and route quality by continuous data collection and sensing;
- real-time map updates for autonomous vehicles;
- road events, e.g., accidents and traffic congestion;
- social applications like BikeNet;
- safety-related and emergency applications (delay sensitive).

Due to delay sensitivity of IoV, the vehicular crowdsensing paradigm is interwoven with edge-/fog-enhanced crowdsourcing. Fog nodes that connect the cloud to end users can be installed on road side units (RSUs) to communicate with vehicles, e.g., through 5G/6G systems. The RSU fog nodes extend the cloud services to the edge, whereas the cloud servers store the history to be utilized later. Another choice for fog nodes includes buses; since they are distributed over urban areas, they are closer to vehicles than RSUs, but they move slower than vehicles. MCS privacy serves as a motivation to vehicles that are usually reluctant to participate in data sharing.

Table 4.2 provides a summary of vehicular MCS security and privacy.

### 4.1.1 Secure fog-based vehicular MCS

The importance of fog-/edge-enhanced MCS in highly mobile vehicular IoV with a need for location awareness is undeniable. Certificateless aggregate signcryption is a technique to enhance information confidentiality, mutual authenticity, and anonymity in fog-based road monitoring.

**Table 4.2** Vehicular MCS security and privacy.

| Goal | Approach | Challenges or evaluation metrics |
|---|---|---|
| Vehicles motivation to provide real-time map updates | Reverse auction incentive mechanism | Limited service platform budget; limited vehicles' resources |
| Security of incentive mechanism and privacy of vehicles | Partially blind signature for secure pseudonym management | Data reliability; task quality of vehicle MCS workers |
| Privacy of incentive mechanism in vehicular MCS | Using buses as fog nodes along with partially blind signature authentication, homomorphic encryption, zero-knowledge verification, and one-way hashing | Feedback delay; reward exchange efficiency |
| Secure distribution of rewards among MCS worker vehicles | Blockchain-based payment; blockchain credit management in which vehicles attach importance to the tasks | Value of services; profit gain |
| Secure information exchange between vehicles and IoT center for emergency (e.g., ambulance carrying a patient) vehicles collaboration | Bidding and incentive mechanisms | Time; success rate |
| Trust in off-chain data in blockchain-based vehicular MCS | Truthful and individually rational reverse auction; data quality evaluation | Social welfare; algorithm scaling with increased number of tasks/mobile nodes; social cost; computational complexity |
| Vehicles' data confidentiality, integrity, mutual authentication, anonymity, and key escrow resilience | Certificateless aggregate signcryption with fog computing; identity-based proxy re-encryption (using random oracle) to ensure security of shared content | Computational cost and communication overhead |

**Table 4.2**    *Continued.*

| Goal | Approach | Challenges or evaluation metrics |
|------|----------|----------------------------------|
| Secure vehicular MCS in-network cache content sharing and distribution with no private information leakage | Use of a trusted content-centric network controller; name function combined with encryption | Varying wireless channel conditions; dynamic network topology |
| No trusted third party against malicious task requestors | Decentralized aggregation in which reputation scores given to MCS workers by the requestors is weighted by the reputation of the requestors | Communication and computation overheads |
| Correlation attack against MCS vehicular social networks | Analyzing the correlation function to determine the sensitive data for suppression | Average processing time; identity/location privacy; information loss |

RSUs (fog nodes) and/or vehicles may become compromised. Therefore, it is safer if the key generation center does not have the MCS participants' full private keys (key escrow resilience).

Filtering out false crowdsensed traffic monitoring data can be handled by data fusion strategies based upon worker vehicles' reputation values. Nevertheless, filtering out such false data becomes particularly challenging when the data is encrypted. One countermeasure is to construct a weighted proximity graph at each fog node through range query in Wi-Fi handshaking.

Anonymous privacy-preserving messages hinder authentication protocols. This is especially dangerous to driver safety in vehicular MCS. Using fog nodes (RSUs) to establish mutual authentication with vehicles prevents the man-in-the-middle attacks.

Although incentive mechanisms comprise an important part of crowdsourcing systems, they may lead to privacy leakage. For example, in reverse auctions, when an MCS worker selects a specific task, its preferences will be revealed. Therefore, the identity of MCS workers should not be linked to their task preferences. To this end, in the token reward generation process, the unique token of a worker is identified using partially blind signature and zero-knowledge authentication techniques before being validated by the fog node. In addition, the worker encrypts the identification code into the crowdsensed data using the public key, so that the fog node cannot track any vehicle.

Malicious MCS workers endanger drivers' safety by providing fraudulent and fake data. As a defense, vehicles need to evaluate the credibility of the senders of crowdsourced data, e.g., through a collaborative crowdsourcing-based reputation scheme. Homomorphic encryption and secure multi-party computation help task requestor vehicles hide their reputation rating/feedback along with the list of MCS workers that provided service to them.

To ensure fairness in computing the aggregate reputation of MCS workers, each task requestor vehicle's provided feedback is given a weight proportional to the trust value of that requestor. To preserve anonymity, the individual reputation ranking of each requestor should not be revealed, but rather the aggregate reputation of vehicles must be provided.

The wireless channel variations and the high speeds of the vehicles make the identity and location privacy protection of vehicles a challenging task. Correlation attacks, such as temporal correlation, spatial correlation, and data correlation, disclose the privacy of participants in crowdsensing-based vehicular social networks. To thwart inference of private information through correlation attacks, mobile management layer and core control layer are added to vehicular MCS systems with three stages including group generation (for $k$-anonymity), identity management, and location suppression. The defense includes a tradeoff between correlation suppression strategies and data loss. This requires analyzing the correlation function and then determining which information is more sensitive to being suppressed.

### 4.1.2 Blockchain-based vehicular MCS

Blockchains and smart contracts are used in MCS IoV for providing trust and incentives in data sharing among vehicles and for secure bidding. Figure 4.1 shows the flow of IoV MCS operation using smart contracts and the blockchain. The crowdsensed task of finding traffic congestion can be automated by the blockchain, e.g., the communications between the vehicles and the IoT center for bidding, payment, and scheduling. All vehicles need to be registered on the blockchain. Each vehicle will offer a bidding price and its data quality, according to task quality metrics published by the IoT center on the blockchain.

Blockchain is a viable solution for trust in on-chain data, whereas data quality-driven reverse auction incentives can ensure trust in off-chain data for the blockchain-based MCS reverse auctions. In a reverse auction, the IoT

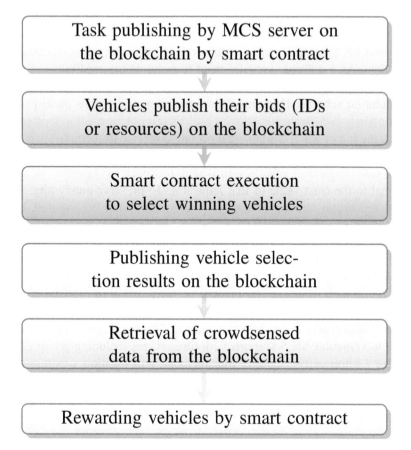

**Figure 4.1**   Vehicular crowdsensing on the blockchain.

center is an auctioneer that purchases data from MCS workers. The auction-based mechanism encourages high-quality sensing data. Another aspect of trust in off-chain data is the data quality evaluation, e.g., via expectation maximization.

To filter out unqualified vehicles from receiving MCS tasks (and rewards), a credit threshold can be managed by the blockchain. This motivates vehicles to improve their credibility by providing high quality crowdsensing data. Moreover, secure pseudonym management based on the partially blind signature can protect the privacy of vehicle MCS workers. The steps of a reputation-based privacy-preserving vehicular MCS may include:

1. encryption of the data of each vehicle (MCS worker) with the ID and parameters of a trusted content-centric networking controller (key generator);
2. collection of encrypted data of vehicles by the task requester;
3. sending the collected crowdsensed data and the desired name function (to calculate the reputation of MCS workers) to the network controller;
4. decrypting the data by the trusted controller who calculates the reputation of each vehicle worker based on the named function;
5. sending the calculated reputation of vehicles by the controller back to the task requester.

### 4.1.3 Sybil attacks on crowdsensed IoV

Crowdsourcing in IoV enables real-time updates about the road map, traffic, etc. (e.g., Waze). Mobile workers continuously send reports about road closures to update the navigation map of vehicles driving toward the reported location. Anonymity and location privacy in crowdsensing can make grounds for sybil attacks.

Pseudonyms, which are based upon public key infrastructure (PKI) or group signatures, do not scale well with the growing number of IoT devices, since the CA cannot handle large numbers of devices. As a remedy, users must be enabled to self-generate an unlimited number of unlinkable pseudonyms, to perform multiple crowdsourcing tasks, without triggering periodic pseudonyms or key renewal from the CA. To prevent sybil attacks, workers should not be allowed to use these pseudonyms for the same task. To implement this type of pseudonymity, sybil attacks on any MCS system (not only IoV) are detected during task subscription by identity-based cryptography, i.e., identity-based signature authentication. A few examples of general defenses against sybil attack include:

- CAPTCHA
- IMEI (International Mobile Equipment Identity) validation of a phone
- Mobile worker device fingerprinting

CAPTCHA loses its effectiveness when attackers use crowdsourced CAPTCHA farms to solve CAPTCHAs in real time. IMEI validation becomes vulnerable when attackers spoof the identifier by fake IMEI generators or public IMEI databases. Device fingerprinting operates by relying on the inherent flaws of mobile sensors (e.g., accelerometers and gyroscopes) upon manufacturing. These intrinsic flaws cause these hardware sensors to generate unique signals that act as device fingerprints. Nevertheless, device fingerprinting may lose authentication accuracy when the number of devices grows very large. Accordingly, not all of the above defenses may be effective for real-time vehicular MCS applications dealing with high speed and low delay requirements.

Sybil attacks are so critical that even a resource-limited device can divert vehicles by creating virtual software-generated (not physically existing) ghost vehicles. Virtual vehicles report false congestion and accidents, without being detected. In crowdsourcing applications for road conditions, traffic, and road mapping, sybil attacks may be launched by emulators (called ghost riders) which remotely send fake traffic hotspots to force cars to divert their route. Sending false GPS updates can mislead crowdsensing applications that use periodic GPS readings from mobile devices to infer traffic speed and road congestion.

For example, full stack mobile emulators (for Android or iOS) can mimic hardware (camera, GPS, etc.). Emulators create virtual mobile devices that do not physically exist. Attackers use these emulators to generate fake GPS location positioning to cause false road congestion alerts. More specifically, by controlling the timing of the GPS updates, the movement speeds of vehicles appear to be slow. This pushes the mobile app to draw a red line on the road on its map, to falsely alert vehicles to change their path for a detour.

A reputation mechanism to verify the validity of road reports can ask vehicles, which are closer to the scene, to send binary votes about the true or false status of a reported road incident. However, sybil emulators may vote in favor of a false road report to outnumber the real votes of physical cars on the road. Specially, since it is easy to create numerous emulated mobile devices, they can easily manipulate the reputation management.

Some real-time MCS mapping and traffic applications allow their users to socialize. A user can send queries to update its information about other users in a particular region. The virtual sybil mobile emulators are able not only to cause traffic congestion (as described before) but also to localize and track other vehicles of interest by launching frequent sybil virtual queries to the server.

For the defense mechanism to such sybil attacks to be viable, it must be established upon the premise of more robust location authentication. This will force the attacker to launch physical devices instead of emulated devices, essentially making the attack more costly and less feasible to be launched.

An important observation in designing the defense is the unlikeliness of sybil emulators to be physically close to real mobile workers. To this end, peer-based mobile worker authentication helps the MCS server to verify if two mobile workers are physically in each other's neighborhood. Wi-Fi signaling appears to be a reasonable choice to implement this peer-based mobile worker authentication.

To implement this defense, the MCS server starts with a few trusted mobile workers[1]. The MCS server provides SSID (service set identifier) to the trusted mobile workers. The trusted mobile workers use this unique SSID to broadcast beacons. The SSID is analogous to the name of the network. Physical devices within the Wi-Fi range receive the beacon and respond by sending the same SSID. As such, trusted nodes propagate the trust on a graph by establishing new edges with newly verified physical devices that drive to their Wi-Fi coverage range.

QUESTION: What is the advantage of choosing Wi-Fi technology for the verification of the physical existence of mobile devices over Bluetooth signaling?

ANSWER: Bluetooth signals have a shorter coverage range than Wi-Fi. This renders Bluetooth signals to be of limited use for the scale of distances among vehicles, especially on larger roads.

When actual physical devices (graph nodes) verify their existence (through Wi-Fi exchange), they form the edges of the graph. The physical devices that meet each other more often have higher weights on the edges that connect them in the graph. As such, actual devices reside on one side of the graph and sybil emulators end up on the other side of this graph, as in Figure 4.2. Weighted edges make it harder for sybil nodes to blend into non-sybil subgraphs. The attacker may be able to bring a few physical devices on the road to juxtapose itself on this graph of trust and falsely verify the legitimacy of its emulators. However, since these falsely authenticated emulators do not come to the physical proximity of other trusted nodes in the graph, they end up at one corner of the graph. Thereby, the attacker will lose the advantage of having numerous emulated devices at its disposal to launch the attack, thus defeating the purpose of sybil attack.

Although the sybil mitigation by proximity graphs form a web of trust, the formation of such graphs requires a certain amount of time. Once the

---

[1] ©[2018] IEEE. Reprinted, with permission, from G. Wang *et al.*, "Ghost Riders: Sybil Attacks on Crowdsourced Mobile Mapping Services," *IEEE/ACM Transactions on Networking*, vol. 26, no. 3, pp. 1123-1136, June 2018

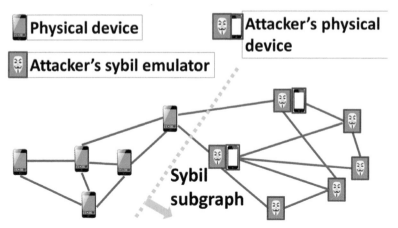

**Figure 4.2**   The graph shows a divide between sybil and physical nodes, since sybil emulated devices do not physically come to the Wi-Fi coverage range of trusted devices.

graph of trust propagation is formed, graph-based sybil detection algorithms can be applied to the graph to rank the nodes based on their legitimacy (physically existing vs. emulated) by considering the weights and sparsity of edges.

### 4.1.4 Future research directions

Example challenges associated with Wi-Fi authenticated formation of the graph of web of trust to identify physical devices from sybil emulators include:

- MCS server needs to have at least one trusted mobile worker on any road, which may not always be feasible on smaller roads or due to vehicles' mobility, unless it is a fixed trusted road side entity.
- Wi-Fi tethering for authentication needs vehicles to be within the Wi-Fi coverage range of each other (e.g., 80 m).
- It takes time to establish the graph to propagate the web of trust. This may hinder it to become an immediate defense mechanism, especially due to high vehicular mobility.
- Even once the graph of trusted physical devices on the road is formed, it can become stale after some time (due to vehicular mobility). The question about the update and maintenance frequency for the graph of trust needs further investigation.

Due to the varying wireless channel conditions and high mobility in the IoV, machine learning methods can be used to predict optimal incentives and fair reward distribution strategies in vehicular MCS.

Another challenge that requires further investigations is when RSU fog nodes are compromised. Since RSU fog nodes send their computational results (collected from potentially false reporting vehicles) to the cloud, the cloud needs mechanisms against untrusted computation results. In general, since fog nodes are closer to MCS workers (compared to remote cloud servers), it is more challenging to preserve location privacy of workers against untrusted fog nodes.

When speed and location of vehicles need to remain private, the vehicles' count may be used to acquire traffic conditions. However, this approach may expose the trajectory of vehicles and, thus, requires further analysis.

## References

M. A. Azad, S. Bag, S. Parkinson, and F. Hao. Trustvote: Privacy-preserving node ranking in vehicular networks. *IEEE Internet of Things Journal*, 6 (4):5878–5891, 2019. doi: 10.1109/JIOT.2018.2880839.

S. Basudan, X. Lin, and K. Sankaranarayanan. A privacy-preserving vehicular crowdsensing-based road surface condition monitoring system using fog computing. *IEEE Internet of Things Journal*, 4(3):772–782, 2017. doi: 10.1109/JIOT.2017.2666783.

W. Chen, Y. Chen, X. Chen, and Z. Zheng. Toward secure data sharing for the iov: A quality-driven incentive mechanism with on-chain and off-chain guarantees. *IEEE Internet of Things Journal*, 7(3):1625–1640, 2020.

C. Lai, M. Zhang, J. Cao, and D. Zheng. SPIR: A secure and privacy-preserving incentive scheme for reliable real-time map updates. *IEEE Internet of Things Journal*, 7(1):416–428, 2020.

C. Li, S. Gong, X. Wang, L. Wang, Q. Jiang, and K. Okamura. Secure and efficient content distribution in crowdsourced vehicular content-centric networking. *IEEE Access*, 6:5727–5739, 2018a.

H. Li, D. Liao, G. Sun, M. Zhang, D. Xu, and Z. Han. Two-stage privacy-preserving mechanism for a crowdsensing-based vsn. *IEEE Access*, 6: 40682–40695, 2018b. doi: 10.1109/ACCESS.2018.2854236.

M. Li, L. Zhu, and X. Lin. Privacy-preserving traffic monitoring with false report filtering via fog-assisted vehicular crowdsensing. *IEEE Transactions on Services Computing*, pages 1–1, 2019. doi: 10.1109/TSC.2019.2903060.

L. Ma, X. Liu, Q. Pei, and Y. Xiang. Privacy-preserving reputation management for edge computing enhanced mobile crowdsensing. *IEEE Transactions on Services Computing*, 12(5):786–799, 2019.

J. Ni, K. Zhang, Y. Yu, X. Lin, and X. S. Shen. Providing task allocation and secure deduplication for mobile crowdsensing via fog computing. *IEEE Transactions on Dependable and Secure Computing*, 17(3):581–594, 2020. doi: 10.1109/TDSC.2018.2791432.

J. Shu, X. Liu, K. Yang, Y. Zhang, X. Jia, and R. H. Deng. Sybsub: Privacy-preserving expressive task subscription with sybil detection in crowdsourcing. *IEEE Internet of Things Journal*, 6(2):3003–3013, 2019. doi: 10.1109/JIOT.2018.2877780.

V. Sucasas, G. Mantas, J. Bastos, F. Damião, and J. Rodriguez. A signature scheme with unlinkable-yet-accountable pseudonymity for privacy-preserving crowdsensing. *IEEE Transactions on Mobile Computing*, 19 (4):752–768, 2020. doi: 10.1109/TMC.2019.2901463.

G. Sun, S. Sun, H. Yu, and M. Guizani. Toward incentivizing fog-based privacy-preserving mobile crowdsensing in the internet of vehicles. *IEEE Internet of Things Journal*, 7(5):4128–4142, 2020. doi: 10.1109/JIOT.2019.2951410.

G. Wang, B. Wang, T. Wang, A. Nika, H. Zheng, and B. Y. Zhao. Ghost riders: Sybil attacks on crowdsourced mobile mapping services. *IEEE/ACM Transactions on Networking*, 26(3):1123–1136, 2018. doi: 10.1109/TNET.2018.2818073. ©[2018] IEEE. Reprinted, with permission.

J. Wei, X. Wang, N. Li, G. Yang, and Y. Mu. A privacy-preserving fog computing framework for vehicular crowdsensing networks. *IEEE Access*, 6:43776–43784, 2018. doi: 10.1109/ACCESS.2018.2861430.

H. Wu, L. Wang, and G. Xue. Privacy-aware task allocation and data aggregation in fog-assisted spatial crowdsourcing. *IEEE Transactions on Network Science and Engineering*, 7(1):589–602, 2020. doi: 10.1109/TNSE.2019.2892583.

B. Yin, Y. Wu, T. Hu, J. Dong, and Z. Jiang. An efficient collaboration and incentive mechanism for internet of vehicles (iov) with secured information exchange based on blockchains. *IEEE Internet of Things Journal*, 7 (3):1582–1593, 2020.

P. Zhou, W. Chen, S. Ji, H. Jiang, L. Yu, and D. Wu. Privacy-preserving online task allocation in edge-computing-enabled massive crowdsensing. *IEEE Internet of Things Journal*, 6(5):7773–7787, 2019. doi: 10.1109/JIOT.2019.2903515.

L. Zhu, M. Li, and Z. Zhang. Secure fog-assisted crowdsensing with collusion resistance: From data reporting to data requesting. *IEEE Internet of Things Journal*, 6(3):5473–5484, 2019. doi: 10.1109/JIOT.2019.2902459.

# 5

## Blockchain-based Solutions for Security and Privacy of MCS Systems

After reading this chapter, you should be able to:

- Combine blockchains with MCS systems.
- Apply smart contracts for secure automation of MCS systems.
- Integrate encryption with blockchain-based MCS.
- Develop reputation management in blockchain-based MCS.

Using the decentralized nature of blockchains and distributed ledgers to impartially record MCS transactions removes dependency on a centralized server. Blockchain nodes can rent out their computing resources to crowdsensing applications for information integrity against misbehaving participants and data aggregation verification. Compared with a traditional MySQL database, integration of MCS with blockchains for data storage and sharing provides higher security and reduces:

1. the cost of a server authority to manage the communications between the requestors and workers;
2. vulnerability to a single point of failure (caused by a centralized server);
3. vulnerability to external attacks, DDoS, DoS, eclipse attack, majority attack, device failure, etc.

MCS participants other than the requester and worker may record services on the blockchain if they have enough power to generate blocks. A recording MCS participant transmits the generated block to other participants to ensure data authenticity. Blockchains detect data tampering since any changes in the blocks are noticed by participants. Data in one block of a blockchain cannot be changed without causing all subsequent blocks to change. The blocks, which encapsulate the data, are linked in order and the information is encrypted using the hash value of the former block, the requestor information,

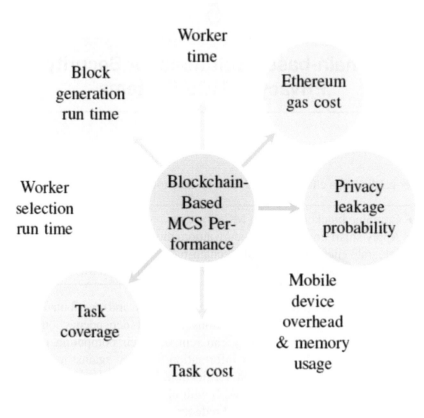

**Figure 5.1** Major performance metrics of blockchain-based MCS.

the worker information, etc. Blockchain offers transparency, and integrity and is used for irrefutable identity verification, identity authentication, and secure tracking of digital identities.

Ethereum is an open-source tamper-proof public ledger blockchain shared by the participating IoT nodes. Ethereum python interface is more accessible than that of Hyperledger. This is due to Hyperledger being designed for storing confidential data (private consortium blockchain), whereas Ethereum is a public blockchain.

Nevertheless, as outlined in Table 5.1, some attack types that can potentially target the crowdsourcing blockchains are:

**Table 5.1** Overview of blockchain-based crowdsourcing privacy and security.

| Problem | Solution |
|---|---|
| Maintain anonymity of blockchain-based MCS mobile users | Elliptic curve algorithm to protect the user identity; user registration without true identity and storing encrypted work in the distributed storage |
| Impersonation, data tampering, repudiation, and denial | Double consensus on the blockchain for node selection using fuzzy theories by calculating the reputation degree and matching degree of each node |
| Validation and block creation of blockchain by the same set of nodes | Separation of transaction validation and block recording between two different groups |
| Protection of user attribute on the public blockchain from association attack/background knowledge attack | Lightweight homomorphic encryption |
| Aggregation of sensing results in the blockchain without exposing original sensing value/sensitive information, e.g., daily routines, personal health, locations, etc. | Additive secret sharing by breaking the requester's secret |
| Lost shares in additive secret sharing due to mobile workers leaving or becoming offline before finishing the task | Delegation to other workers based on local and global reputation scores; breaking the secret share of the abandoned worker among delegate workers |
| Data quality and reliability evaluation | Reputation evaluation based on data distortion, data consistency, local rating, and contextual factors |
| Disclosure of a requester's feedback about a worker on the public blockchain | Two-stage local/global reputation by updating and publishing the reputation scores only after a group of requestors have provided their feedback |
| DDoS, sybil, collusion, false reporting, and free riding attacks (malicious workers) | Payment of deposit before participation; allowing the consensus amongst a trusted subgroup of nodes to represent the consensus of the nodes in the whole network (proposed consensus implemented on Windows 8 with an i7 Intel Core CPU and 32-GB RAM) |

**Table 5.1**   *Continued.*

| Problem | Solution |
|---|---|
| Subjective third-party task evaluation prevention; transparent monetization | Smart contracts; automatic reward delivery on the blockchain for crowdsourced knowledge monetization (implemented on Amazon AWS EC2 cloud and Ethereum) |
| Trust in off-chain data | Data quality estimation based on EM algorithm to learn the actual task data from the data submitted by MCS workers |
| Miners violating participants' privacy by impersonation attacks | Node grouping for $k$-anonymity; secure incentive mechanism |
| Eclipse attack, majority attack, terminal device failure, and transaction forgery | Certificate authority to review authenticity and data ownership and manage the public keys of mobile terminals based on the assumption of a private chain owning honest mining nodes (implemented on Geth 1.7.2 (Go Ethereum), on the Ubuntu 16.04 LTS with Intel Core 3.40 GHz i7-6700 CPU and 16-GB RAM) |
| Privacy during task matching including: workers' preferences, identity anonymity of workers/requesters/task requirements, and reliable task matching according to workers' preferences | Blockchain to store the encrypted index; combining smart contracts with searchable encryption on Ethereum (with metrics of gas and worker time costs) |

- Sybil attack in which the attacker creates many accounts to gain majority in the blockchain consensus. As a countermeasure, the MCS consensus validators need to be chosen based on their trust/reputation scores.
- Collusion among requestors and miners or among workers and miners. Reward and punishment mechanism can mitigate collusion by rewarding faithful nodes with service coins as a transaction fee. Colluding nodes may be punished by lower trust or reputation values.
- Distributed denial of service (DDoS): Some nodes may flood the blockchain communication by sending too many transactions. To prevent DDoS messages, every message needs to be signed by its transmitter. Traffic cleansing devices and mandating a fee for each transaction can defend against DDoS.

## 5.1 Miners in MCS

Miners can be additional participants in blockchain-based MCS (not necessarily eliminating the server) but replacing the server to evaluate the quality of workers' task submissions. The miners' role is to verify transactions between workers and requestors and to compile them into blocks. Data is inspected by the miners, instead of being verified by the centralized controller, as a security solution against an untrusted server. Miners use an evaluation function provided by the requester to evaluate and confirm the quality of submitted work for task solution performed by the worker. This leads to measuring and updating reputation of workers and more rewards are provided to superior workers. The expectation maximization algorithm and mutual information are used among miners. Some nodes in the blockchain are nominators, i.e., only responsible for receiving and broadcasting data sharing transaction requests. Compared to a miner, a nominator requires less computation resources.

The server publishes a task along with its quality evaluation criteria and deposits the reward on the blockchain. The deposit is to secure the reward for workers who finish the task according to the server's quality criteria. However, to eliminate server's free riding, mobile workers do not submit their task directly to the server but first to the peer-to-peer network for evaluation. Through a set of predefined smart contracts, the miners verify the identities of MCS participants and validate the sensing procedure before the reward allocation. After validation, the task's data is given to the server while the corresponding hash digests are saved in the peer-to-peer network to remove any doubts about the miners' validation. Workers whose work has met the criteria will receive their rewards from the server through extended Bitcoin transaction syntax pricing in accordance with the reward transfer conditions in the transaction script. The transaction script further contains information about the workers who submit a task and their quality. Since this can jeopardize workers' privacy, the miners are assigned to evaluate tasks from a group of workers so that miners cannot distinguish the work of any individual in that group. To defend against *impersonation attacks by miners*, who may direct the payment to themselves, the transaction verification uses commutative encryptions. To avoid the need for hiring extra miners, workers can choose to become either miners or workers, but only one of these roles at a time.

## 5.2 Smart Contracts in MCS

Smart contracts are a mechanism for secure automation of the main functionalities of MCS. Examples such as task posting, worker selection, task allocation, task receiving, task execution, reward assignment, and reward payment can be implemented by smart contracts (e.g., on Ethereum public test network).

Three examples of smart contract types for MCS are (a) user register smart contract, (b) user summary smart contract, and (c) requester–worker relationship contract. The evaluation of tasks can be performed via smart contract as a countermeasure against free-riding requestors and unreliable task solutions provided by unreliable workers.

Worker selection is automated by a smart contract to find workers for tasks published by requestors. This type of smart contract should reliably meet the interests of workers, the requirements of the tasks, data confidentiality, and identity anonymity. When a task has multiple requestors, session key for each task can preserve confidentiality. Inverted index for encrypted keyword search in the smart contract is a computationally efficient method to protect anonymity and the privacy of task requirements and workers' preferences. In this scheme:

- The task requester uploads the task through a one-task-only blockchain address to prevent revealing the identity.
- The worker retrieves the task by querying the read-only function of the blockchain without revealing the query or identity.
- The query cannot be linked to the worker identity by searchable encryption in the smart contract.

## 5.3 Encryption in Blockchain-based MCS

Transparent public blockchains lack privacy. Moreover, malicious MCS participants may misbehave by providing invalid data or invalid data aggregation. Asymmetric encryption in the digital signature allows the blockchain to verify if a transaction was signed by the correct private key, thereby protecting MCS participants against external attacks. The task requester provides a public key to workers to encrypt their aggregated data to prevent plagiarism on the open transparent blockchain. MCS participants use their private key for their signature. To broadcast a task, the requester posts its digital signature and public key and generates a hash digest of all task requirements. This requires the requestor to be trusted, however.

Users in a decentralized blockchain-based MCS can register without their true identity (to preserve their privacy) and store encrypted solutions in the distributed storage. To thwart DDoS, sybil, and false-reporting security attacks, each identity is required to deposit a fee before participation, which can be negligible compared to high service fees demanded by a centralized server.

Another application of the cryptocurrency built on blockchains is to securely motivate MCS workers. High-quality skilled workers are rewarded with payments that are recorded in transaction blocks. $k$-anonymity privacy is achieved through node cooperation verification. The node cooperation-based privacy mechanism hides private information in a group to deal with impersonation attacks in the open and transparent blockchain. Workers and requestors can use signcryption as a privacy countermeasure against disclosure to the miners. Signcryption is faster than sequential signature and encryption.

The smart contract will automatically select qualified workers among the pre-registered workers and send back the deposit to non-selected workers. After completing the task, workers store their signed encrypted data in the distributed database (along with their public key) and wait for the evaluation of the task requester. The qualified workers receive their payment after the evaluation stage. The challenge is designing a fair evaluation mechanism that prevents free-riding attack by requestors. To measure the run times of block generation, worker selection, task coverage, and task cost, this NP-hard optimization problem has been implemented on Ethereum using Python 3.5 on 2.60-GHz Core (TM) i7-6700HQ CPU, 20.00-GB, Windows 10 64 bit.

In the above schemes, recording public keys on the blockchain and encrypting the data under each recorded public key incurs on-chain storage overhead and monetary costs, e.g., on Ethereum. Additionally, the size of the uploaded ciphertexts increases with the number of MCS participants. Since the storage space on the blockchain is limited, an off-chain distributed database may be used as an accessory. Due to the cost of on-chain processing, it is uneconomical for all of the workload to be on-chain. Hence, a balance must be maintained between on-chain and off-chain deployments. Turing-complete programming languages handle complex crowdsourcing logics and increase crowdsourcing flexibility.

Workers may obtain their public and private keys by registering through a certificate authority (CA) for data privacy in the public Ethereum-based mobile crowdsourcing. The public key can identify the user in blockchain and the signature cannot be forged without the user's private key. Workers encrypt data with their private key before sending it to the CA. The CA checks whether the received data is from a previously registered worker. The role of the trusted key manager (or CA) is protection against data authenticity and ownership forgery caused by the open nature of Ethereum. After verification, the signature of CA is sent back to the worker before the worker stores its encrypted data and CA's signature verification on the blockchain. The network ID, system mining difficulty, and gas limit are among the parameters that need to be set up in the genesis block. Operations such as block query, transactions, and mining can be simulated via JavaScript Console launched by Ethereum nodes. The smart contract may be implemented in the Solidity language, which includes initialization of the MCS workers' accounts, their storage function, etc.

Since crowdsensed data on the blockchain is encrypted for privacy, verifying the truthfulness of this data in the cloud can be done by independent servers through lightweight cryptographic additive secret sharing. More specifically, workers encrypt executed tasks by splitting the data into secret shares. Each cloud server receives one share without knowing the shares of other servers. The cloud servers then process the data using the weight of each worker. MCS data confidentiality implies the data is not revealed to MCS participants and cloud servers and it is revealed to the requestor only after the completion of monetization.

After the cloud servers verify the reliability against falsified data, the blockchain comes into operation to automate a tamper-proof MCS monetization. The blockchain nodes can form a secret-managing committee of trustees. The smart contract specifically records the identities of requesters who have paid for the crowdsourced data. A group of Ethereum blockchain nodes then securely deliver the crowdsourced data to authorized requestors. This scheme is implemented on Amazon AWS EC2 cloud and the Ethereum blockchain. Nevertheless, the premise of additive secret sharing is that servers do not collude to share secrets with each other. Otherwise, this method fails to preserve privacy in the cloud.

In a fair marketplace for selling the data produced by MCS workers to requestors, the workers are rewarded once the cloud servers verify the truth about data against falsified information.

## 5.4 Consensus Protocols in Blockchain MCS

A major challenge in adopting blockchains in MCS is the design of a suitable consensus protocol. The Bitcoin's proof-of-work (PoW) mining suffers low throughput and demands resources. Paxos-based and Byzantine fault tolerance family of algorithms suffer scalability issues with larger numbers of IoT crowdsourcing participants and might not handle all types of unfaithful behaviors. The proof-of-stake (PoS) lacks fairness by giving easier mining puzzles to richer participants. Another drawback of PoS is that block generators have nothing to lose by voting for multiple blockchain histories, which may cause the consensus to never resolve. Charging a cost for working on multiple chains can be a solution.

On the contrary, the proof-of-trust (PoT) consensus balances between security and fairness by assigning the transaction validation and block recording to two different sets of blockchain nodes. This contrasts with a traditional blockchain, where the validation and the block creation of the consensus are conducted by the same set of nodes. Its architecture includes a private consortium that includes a crowdsourcing site operator, regulators, notaries, etc. Each consortium member has a consortium ledger management node and a gateway node. The ledger management nodes are responsible for selecting validators from the open crowdsourcing platform. The gateway nodes isolate private information of the private consortium from the Internet while communicating to validators.

The validators in the public crowdsourcing platform (selected by the ledger management nodes residing in the private consortium) send their majority consensus on the transactions to the gateway. The gateway then passes the consensus to the ledger management nodes who vote on the transactions chosen by the majority of the validators as another layer of trust. The leader of the ledger management nodes (selected by Raft leader selection method) creates the transaction block and broadcasts it to the consortium blockchain. In Raft consensus, a leader is elected among the nodes, and all updates go through the leader, simplifying the algorithm's implementation. In contrast, Paxos is more decentralized, without a distinct leader, and relies on a multi-round voting process for reaching consensus.

The PoT consensus selects transaction validators based on their trust values to mitigate sybil attack, collusion, or DDoS. Dual ledgers and dual consensus protocols integrate a public chain, running the delegated proof-of-stake consensus, and subchains, running the practical Byzantine fault tolerance consensus. This allows them to outperform Casper consensus in Ethereum by achieving higher transaction throughput and less execution time compared with traditional PoW/PoS-based blockchain.

## 5.5  MCS Workers' Location Privacy on the Public Blockchain

The location of MCS workers may be revealed at the worker selection stage. The worker's account may contain the travel limitations for location-based crowdsourcing tasks. A spatial anonymous area around the true location (called cloaked area) can preserve the location privacy in MCS.

A task requester and a worker anonymously pre-register by uploading their information and submitting a deposit to create their accounts on the blockchain to post tasks. The deposit to sign a smart contract with the task requester prevents sybil attacks.

## 5.6  MCS Reputation Management on the Blockchain

Reputation management against MCS participants who provide false data can also be left to the blockchain that replaces a malicious centralized server.

To protect private information of MCS participants (sensing data, aggregation result, requester's feedback, etc.), the blockchain and edge computing are integrated on the Hyperledger Sawtooth and Android client. To eliminate inaccurate ratings by malicious requestors, the two main steps of reputation management consist of:

- local reputation evaluation in which the data reliability is evaluated by the requesters' positive or negative rating of the worker's data;
- global reputation update in which the global reputation scores are updated by the smart contract based on the average of the ratings from requesters.

The role of the blockchain public ledger in this case is to transparently store the global reputation of MCS workers. However, any new rating of a worker's reputation submitted by a requestor leaks the variation in reputation in a public manner, which violates anonymity. One solution is to refrain from updating the global reputation on the blockchain until after at least a batch of requestors submit their reputation scores. Additionally, additive secret sharing for global reputation update on the blockchain protects the reputation scores from being revealed. Nevertheless, additive secret sharing is challenging when some mobile workers leave or become off-line before they complete the sensing task. Due to the lost shares, the secret key cannot be reconstructed. A solution is that the sensing task of an off-line worker is to be delegated to a set of on-line workers, which are selected according to their local or global reputation scores.

## 5.7 Future Research Directions

Blockchain technology, which is still in its early stages, is suffering from limitations, such as:

- computational costs of mining;
- recursive calling vulnerability, timestamp dependence, arithmetic problem, and return value problem;
- computationally intensive consensus mechanisms;
- collusions involving miners, e.g., between an anonymity group and miners, miners and the server, and MCS participants and miners;
- distributed denial-of-service attacks and theft of content;
- increased latency with the number of IoT nodes in blockchain MCS.

The liveness guarantee of the consensus protocol (due to Fischer, Lynch, and Paterson or FLP impossibility), consensus deadlock, and applications of game theory still need more investigation. Evaluation functions provided by the requester need to be revisited since the requester may not know about the solution characteristics beforehand.

## References

Editorial: Blockchain in industrial iot applications: Security and privacy advances, challenges, and opportunities. *IEEE Transactions on Industrial Informatics*, 16(6):4119–4121, 2020.

J. An, H. Yang, X. Gui, W. Zhang, R. Gui, and J. Kang. Tcns: Node selection with privacy protection in crowdsensing based on twice consensuses of blockchain. *IEEE Transactions on Network and Service Management*, 16 (3):1255–1267, 2019.

Chengjun Cai, Yifeng Zheng, Yuefeng Du, Zhan Qin, and Cong Wang. Towards private, robust, and verifiable crowdsensing systems via public blockchains. *IEEE Transactions on Dependable and Secure Computing*, 18(4):1893–1907, 2021a. doi: 10.1109/TDSC.2019.2941481.

Chengjun Cai, Yifeng Zheng, Anxin Zhou, and Cong Wang. Building a secure knowledge marketplace over crowdsensed data streams. *IEEE Transactions on Dependable and Secure Computing*, 18(6):2601–2616, 2021b. doi: 10.1109/TDSC.2019.2958901.

W. Chen, Y. Chen, X. Chen, and Z. Zheng. Toward secure data sharing for the iov: A quality-driven incentive mechanism with on-chain and off-chain guarantees. *IEEE Internet of Things Journal*, 7(3):1625–1640, 2020.

Arthur Gervais, Ghassan O. Karame, Karl Wüst, Vasileios Glykantzis, Hubert Ritzdorf, and Srdjan Capkun. On the security and performance of proof of work blockchains. In *ACM SIGSAC Conference on Computer and Communications Security*, pages 3–16, 2016.

J. Hu, K. Yang, K. Wang, and K. Zhang. A blockchain-based reward mechanism for mobile crowdsensing. *IEEE Transactions on Computational Social Systems*, 7(1):178–191, 2020.

M. Li, J. Weng, A. Yang, W. Lu, Y. Zhang, L. Hou, J. Liu, Y. Xiang, and R. H. Deng. Crowdbc: A blockchain-based decentralized framework for crowdsourcing. *IEEE Transactions on Parallel and Distributed Systems*, 30(6):1251–1266, 2019.

C. H. Liu, Q. Lin, and S. Wen. Blockchain-enabled data collection and sharing for industrial IoT with deep reinforcement learning. *IEEE Transactions on Industrial Informatics*, 15(6):3516–3526, 2019.

J. Wang, M. Li, Y. He, H. Li, K. Xiao, and C. Wang. A blockchain based privacy-preserving incentive mechanism in crowdsensing applications. *IEEE Access*, 6:17545–17556, 2018.

Y. Wu, S. Tang, B. Zhao, and Z. Peng. Bptm: Blockchain-based privacy-preserving task matching in crowdsourcing. *IEEE Access*, 7:45605–45617, 2019.

X. Xu, Q. Liu, X. Zhang, J. Zhang, L. Qi, and W. Dou. A blockchain-powered crowdsourcing method with privacy preservation in mobile environment. *IEEE Transactions on Computational Social Systems*, 6(6):1407–1419, 2019.

K. Zhao, S. Tang, B. Zhao, and Y. Wu. Dynamic and privacy-preserving reputation management for blockchain-based mobile crowdsensing. *IEEE Access*, 7:74694–74710, 2019.

S. Zhu, Z. Cai, H. Hu, Y. Li, and W. Li. zkcrowd: A hybrid blockchain-based crowdsourcing platform. *IEEE Transactions on Industrial Informatics*, 16 (6):4196–4205, 2020.

J. Zou, B. Ye, L. Qu, Y. Wang, M. A. Orgun, and L. Li. A proof-of-trust consensus protocol for enhancing accountability in crowdsourcing services. *IEEE Transactions on Services Computing*, 12(3):429–445, 2019.

S. Zou, J. Xi, H. Wang, and G. Xu. Crowdblps: A blockchain-based location-privacy-preserving mobile crowdsensing system. *IEEE Transactions on Industrial Informatics*, 16(6):4206–4218, 2020.

# 6

# MCS Security Games and Incentive Mechanisms

After reading this chapter, you should be able to:

- Apply game-theory methods for MCS security.
- Distinguish between the applications of auctions and reverse auctions in MCS.
- Select incentive mechanisms for truthful MCS.
- Compose steps toward stable task assignment in MCS.

Table 6.1 and Figure 6.1 showcase the major use of game theory and incentive mechanisms for the protection of MCS systems.

## 6.1 MCS Games

Game theory can trigger cooperation among selfish users. The interactions between the requestor and a worker can be modeled as an iterative two-player prisoner's dilemma game. Rewarding/penalizing a worker's cooperation/non-cooperation incentivizes cooperative behavior. In this regard, the requestor changes the expected payoff of the worker based on zero-determinant strategies, i.e., offering the worker more short-term payoff without sacrificing the long-term interest of the requestor. However, a free-riding requestor may penalize a cooperative worker to gain profit. In such a case, the worker needs to adopt an evolutionary strategy to enforce fair cooperation in an iterative prisoner's dilemma game. Solutions based on evolutionary game theory for reputation update can be used against free riding and false reporting. In this framework, the interaction between the worker and the requester is modeled as an asymmetric gift-giving game with different strategy sets for task requestors and workers.

**Table 6.1** Game theory and truthful incentive mechanisms for MCS privacy and security.

| Problem | Solution |
|---|---|
| Profit maximization among MCS players, i.e., monthly paid workers, task requestors, and instant-paid workers | Design of three two-player Stackelberg subgames and using backward induction to find the equilibria of Stackelberg games |
| Maximizing the social welfare under lack of cooperation and myopic equilibrium | Two-sided rating with differential punishments of MCS users with different ratings |
| Balancing individual privacy and data utility under time-varying privacy demands | Noncooperative differential game and dynamic programming to obtain Nash equilibrium |
| • Reducing privacy leakage of MCS data uploading and trading<br>• Balancing data accuracy and privacy sensitivity, i.e., cumulative difference between the prior and the posterior probabilities | • Three party games among 1) mobile workers, 2) edge nodes, and 3) cloud MCS server<br>• Game tree to observe the behavioral strategies of players and to model payoff functions |
| Free-riding and false-reporting attacks | Evolutionary game theory for reputation update |
| Mobile worker privacy in individually rational and truthful incentive mechanisms for crowdsourced indoor localization using continuous time-varying Wi-Fi signals (as opposed to one-shot sensing) | • Two-stage Stackelberg game to maximize mobile worker utility and MCS server profit<br>• Differential privacy with joint optimization of the variable reward for mobile workers (when MCS server knows each mobile user's sensitivity level of data privacy); a demand function model for the relationships among MCS server, mobile workers, and service customers<br>• *Age of data* freshness metric (the time passed since the last generation of the data) to determine the rewards in the reverse auction incentive mechanism |
| Sybil attacks in auction-based MCS under the assumption of no monopoly mobile worker | Breaking the bid from each mobile user into atomic bids for one task only and paying $(n+1)$th smallest value to the $n$ winning bids |
| Simultaneous MCS data trustworthiness, user privacy, and incentive fairness without a trusted third party | Anonymous trust/reputation and cryptographic protocols to enable benign MCS users to request tasks, contribute data, and earn rewards anonymously without data linkability |

**Table 6.1** *Continued.*

| Problem | Solution |
|---|---|
| Bid privacy against inference attack in VCG (Vickrey-Clarke-Groves) auction-based MCS for worker recruitment and optimal task assignment, while minimizing social cost | • Secure group bidding for disguising the bids within the groups<br>• Lagrange polynomial interpolation to perturb workers' bids within groups<br>• Differentially private exponential mechanism to limit the impact of a worker's bid change on the auction outcome |
| Reputation update in ciphertext domain | Adding a separate reputation manager to the crowdsensing system; somewhat homomorphic encryption (SHE) and DGK comparison protocol to rank the reputations |

The three-subgame Stackelberg game is an incentive mechanism through which the MCS participants can calculate the strategies that will maximize their profit (profit evaluation smart contract). The Stackelberg game is based on a leader and a follower. The first movers in the Stackelberg game crowdsourcing market are monthly paid workers who dominate the market. When the subgame has Nash equilibrium, the follower's strategy is optimal given the leader's strategy. Followers play the game with strategies that are informed by the strategy and preferences of the leader until reaching an optimum. In the first subgame, the leader is the monthly paid MCS worker while the follower is the task requestor. In the second subgame, the leader is the task requester, and the followers are the instant-paid workers. In the third noncooperative subgame, the players are instant-paid MCS workers. Backward induction finds the equilibria of the subgames.

A noncooperative differential game model can balance the tradeoff between contradictory goals of individual privacy and ensuring data utility under time-varying users' privacy demands. The feedback Nash equilibrium, wherein MCS participants and the server achieve maximum privacy and data utility, may be obtained by dynamic programming. Lack of cooperation among self-interested users does cause a service exchange dilemma with zero social welfare obtained at myopic equilibrium. Two-stage game model for two-sided rating can overcome the inefficiency of the socially undesirable equilibrium and maximize the social welfare by the optimal choice of parameters that affect users' behaviors and users' valuation of their long-term utilities. To address anonymous MCS requestors with asymmetric service requirements and workers' different service capabilities, the game theoretic

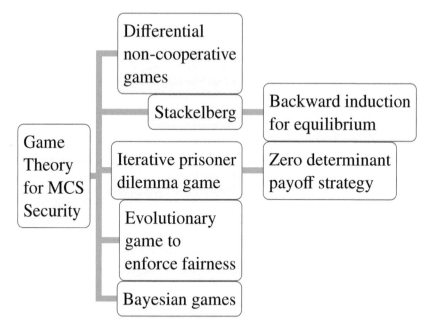

**Figure 6.1**   Game theory methods for MCS security.

two-sided rating with differential punishment applies different punishments for MCS users who have different ratings. To this end, strategy recommendation selects a desirable behavior from predefined plans while participants update their ratings according to a rating update rule.

## 6.2 Robust Incentive Mechanisms for MCS

Mobile IoT crowdsourcing systems are a type of sensory data market. Similar to any market, they need to be fair and provide incentive mechanisms. Incentive mechanisms motivate the participation of mobile workers in crowdsourcing tasks. The three main elements in Figure 6.2, major incentive mechanisms for establishing trust in MCS, can be combined to increase reliability.

### 6.2.1 Reputation schemes

Malicious participants can be detected by a reputation mechanism, by grouping participants, and constantly updating the trust value. The reputation of

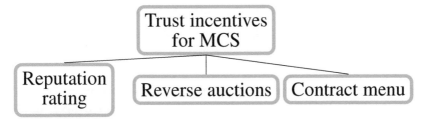

**Figure 6.2**    Major incentive mechanisms toward trustworthy MCS.

each participant is updated based on the deviation of the participant's result from the aggregated result or an evaluation function provided by the task requestor. This deviation calculation can be performed in the encrypted domain by considering the difference between participant's encrypted result and the encrypted aggregated result. To overcome free-riding and false-reporting attacks, truthful evolutionary games can inform the design of intelligent reputation update incentive mechanisms by predicting the evolution of MCS systems. A motivation for workers to provide truthful data is various reputation thresholds, which are dynamically adjusted for various tasks to avoid excessive punishment of potential truthful workers.

To enable the simultaneous goals of incentive fairness, data trustworthiness, and MCS user privacy, anonymous trust or reputation models allow legitimate users to join tasks anonymously and obtain rewards while preventing malicious users. To hinder the abuse of anonymity, the number of issued pseudonyms should be limited.

Updating the reputation of a mobile worker, based on the deviations of its sensed data from the aggregated results, exposes the deviation to the MCS server. To conceal this deviation, a separate reputation manager is added to the crowdsensing system and somewhat homomorphic encryption (SHE) scheme is used, which allows processing of ciphertext without having to decrypt it. The following steps protect the actual deviations from colluding nodes:

1. The task requestor asks the certificate authority (CA) to generate public and private keys.
2. The task request and the public key are sent to the cloud MCS server to be distributed to mobile workers (via edge nodes).
3. Mobile workers send their encrypted sensing results to edge nodes.
4. The edge nodes calculate the encrypted deviations and apply the DGK comparison protocol for the reputation manager to obtain the rank of the deviations.

5. The reputation manager uses the rank of deviations to update the reputations of workers.

## 6.2.2 Auctions for truthfulness in mobile crowdsourcing

Auctions and payment determination are tools to motivate truthful behavior among MCS participants by minimizing the cost incurred upon task requestors and maximizing the benefit of workers. Auctions need to be individually rational, budget-balanced, and computationally efficient. Threats against auction-based MCS systems include:

- false-name or sybil attacks on auctions to increase the utilities of malicious users;
- collusion attacks;
- bid privacy leakage of smartphone users by chosen plaintext attack;
- location privacy leakage of bidding mobile workers.

As a countermeasure against sybil attacks, auctions need to be designed in a way that each user is better off not generating any false names. Core selecting-based incentive mechanisms integrate auctions into MCS to incentivize truthfulness. Vickrey-Clarke-Groves (VCG) auctions are used to provide the maximum gain for users who reveal the real value of their bid based on their location and time. MCS participants are assumed to be only aware of their own bid and not of the other bidders (no collusion). To incentivize truthful bids, the reward is the second lowest bid in VCG auctions.

## 6.2.3 Reverse auction for MCS task assignment

Since crowdsourcing tasks demand consumption of workers' device resources, selfish MCS workers prefer to save their limited resources (e.g., energy, storage, and computation capacity) rather than exhausting them on the assigned task. Incentive methods based on reverse auction games motivate MCS workers to complete a crowdsourced task. The reverse auction task assignment needs to incorporate truthfulness, individual rationality, efficiency in computation/communication, and privacy protection for workers. However, the winning bid selection in the reverse auction task assignment can be an NP-hard problem, e.g., when it is modeled as an $n$-to-one weighted bipartite graph matching with multiple binary knapsack constraints. As a remedy, approximation algorithms are used to select winning bids and determine payments.

Task assignment for crowdsourcing needs to address the conflicting goals of maximizing the utility of the MCS platform, minimizing the cost of requesters, satisfaction of requestors and workers, truthfulness, individual rationality, and stability. Game theory deals with the satisfaction of both workers and requestor, whereas intelligent matching results in stability. The steps toward a stable task assignment and matching include:

1. The MCS server asks the requesters and workers, separately, to describe their individual requirements and preferences using a multi-attribute information structure.
2. The MCS server collects the multi-attribute information and rewards for the tasks from requestors and workers, respectively.
3. Tasks are assigned to mobile workers based on matching the multi-attribute structures of both parties.
4. The integrated satisfaction degrees of both requestors and workers with respect to their published multiple attributes are calculated.
5. The satisfaction degree is used for pricing and payment through a second-price reverse auction mechanism.

### 6.2.4 Bid privacy in auction-based MCS

The bids of MCS participants may include private information, e.g., spatial locations and routes, leading to inference attacks. Preserving the bid privacy of smartphone MCS workers while minimizing the social cost in auction-based incentive crowdsourcing can be achieved by semantic disguise of each user bidding for a set of desired tasks followed by selecting users based on score functions (e.g., linear and log functions). The bid disguise guarantees cipher text indistinguishably against chosen-plain-text attack, since no statistical information can be gained from the bid. To this end, the key generator distributes a series of polynomial outcomes and IDs to mobile workers, which they use to disguise their original bid value. A third-party data aggregator then calculates the minimum bid among all participants' bids without knowing each participant's actual bid value.

### 6.2.5 Incentives via contract menu

When the MCS server is not trusted, MCS workers prefer to randomly add calibrated noise to their sensing data before reporting to preserve their privacy. This, in turn, degrades the quality of task completion. In such cases, contracts can characterize the workers' equilibrium behavior toward maximizing the accuracy of data aggregation under budget constraints. A contract menu offers different contracts to MCS workers to accommodate their varying privacy levels without each worker's precise privacy preference being revealed to the MCS server. The contract menu, designed with incomplete information, determines the payment to MCS workers to incentivize them to give up some of their differential privacy. The incomplete information contract leverages the probability distribution of worker' privacy preferences to quantify the impact of each worker's privacy on task accuracy.

## 6.3 Integration of Differential Privacy with Mechanism Design for Mobile Crowdsourcing

While auctions aim to maximize the revenue and guarantee truthfulness, differential privacy protects the privacy in the data collection phase. Integration of auctions with differentially-private data pricing/collection prevents the leakage of identity of requestors to workers and vice versa. Moreover, differentially-private mechanism design enables each MCS participant to hide its cost, as the MCS participants and the server each aim to maximize their benefits with constrained device resources. For example, in Wi-Fi-based indoor localization to construct radio maps, incentive mechanisms are combined with differential privacy. The interaction between MCS workers and the server is a two-stage Stackelberg game to maximize the utility of both workers and the server.

   Mobile workers are able to hide their exact locations if they form groups and select a group master to collect and report their differentially private and randomized sensing reports. The selection process of the group master leans itself to a non-cooperative Bayesian game model and the Bayes–Nash equilibrium. The utility of the players (i.e., MCS workers) is their privacy gain. Due to the inherent noise in differentially private MCS, the notion of auction truthfulness is replaced with expected truthfulness.

### 6.3.1 Future research directions

Although monetary rewards are encouraging incentives for workers, they cannot prevent denial-of-payment (free riding) attacks by malicious task requestors. Even worse, malicious workers may launch data pollution, sybil, and replacement attacks. As a countermeasure, data reliability must be measured based on the deviation of the data from ground truth, while preserving the anonymity and location privacy of mobile workers.

Some areas of further exploration include:

- taking into account the capability variance of task participants into the design of the privacy-preserving incentive mechanisms;
- device-to-device or peer-to-peer communication to save the cost and energy in the spatial coverage of crowdsourced fingerprint collection;
- investigating the tradeoff between privacy and task quality to incentivize mobile workers;
- exploring various score functions (other than linear and log) to achieve differential privacy and proximate social cost minimization;
- utility-maximizing incentive mechanisms combined with novel data aggregation and data perturbation against linking attacks on privacy;
- extension of two-sided rating protocols from two-level rating to multiple levels, as well as optimal selection of the size of the rating labels and the threshold value for users' punishment or reward;
- reinforcement learning for the optimal continuous rating labels/continuous MCS server actions;
- study of the game models on the blockchain, for privacy-preserving intelligent matching between task requesters and mobile workers;
- repeated game behaviors to capture multiple rounds of interaction among MCS entities in the design of the payoff function, and measuring the risk of data privacy leakage;
- extension of multi-attribute task assignment to the case when each task can be completed by more than one worker, and each requestor has more than one task at a given time;
- mitigation of the impacts of collusion among mobile workers on the cooperation probabilities of both the task requestor and the workers in zero-determinant-based incentive mechanisms for multiple-player games.

## References

G. Gao, M. Xiao, J. Wu, S. Zhang, L. Huang, and G. Xiao. Dpdt: A differentially private crowd-sensed data trading mechanism. *IEEE Internet of Things Journal*, 7(1):751–762, 2020. doi: 10.1109/JIOT.2019.2944107.

H. Gao, H. Xu, L. Zhang, and X. Zhou. A differential game model for data utility and privacy-preserving in mobile crowdsensing. *IEEE Access*, 7: 128526–128533, 2019. doi: 10.1109/ACCESS.2019.2940096.

K. Han, H. Liu, S. Tang, M. Xiao, and J. Luo.   Differentially private mechanisms for budget limited mobile crowdsourcing.   *IEEE
Transactions on Mobile Computing*, 18(4):934–946, 2019.   doi:
10.1109/TMC.2018.2848265.

J. Hu, H. Lin, X. Guo, and J. Yang. Dtcs: An integrated strategy for enhancing
data trustworthiness in mobile crowdsourcing. *IEEE Internet of Things
Journal*, 5(6):4663–4671, 2018.

J. Hu, K. Yang, K. Wang, and K. Zhang. A blockchain-based reward mechanism for mobile crowdsensing. *IEEE Transactions on Computational
Social Systems*, 7(1):178–191, 2020a.

Q. Hu, S. Wang, X. Cheng, L. Ma, and R. Bie.   Solving the crowdsourcing dilemma using the zero-determinant strategies. *IEEE Transactions
on Information Forensics and Security*, 15:1778–1789, 2020b.   doi:
10.1109/TIFS.2019.2949440.

P. Huang, X. Zhang, L. Guo, and M. Li.   Incentivizing crowdsensing-
based noise monitoring with differentially-private locations.   *IEEE
Transactions on Mobile Computing*, 20(2):519–532, 2021.   doi:
10.1109/TMC.2019.2946800.

T. Li, T. Jung, Z. Qiu, H. Li, L. Cao, and Y. Wang.   Scalable
privacy-preserving participant selection for mobile crowdsensing systems: Participant grouping and secure group bidding. *IEEE Transactions on Network Science and Engineering*, 7(2):855–868, 2020a. doi:
10.1109/TNSE.2018.2791948.

W. Li, C. Zhang, Z. Liu, and Y. Tanaka.   Incentive mechanism design for
crowdsourcing-based indoor localization. *IEEE Access*, 6:54042–54051,
2018. doi: 10.1109/ACCESS.2018.2869202.

W. Li, C. Zhang, and Y. Tanaka.   Privacy-aware sensing-quality-
based budget feasible incentive mechanism for crowdsourcing fingerprint collection.   *IEEE Access*, 8:49775–49784, 2020b.   doi:
10.1109/ACCESS.2020.2974909.

J. Lin, D. Yang, M. Li, J. Xu, and G. Xue. Frameworks for privacy-preserving
mobile crowdsensing incentive mechanisms. *IEEE Transactions on Mobile
Computing*, 17(8):1851–1864, 2018. doi: 10.1109/TMC.2017.2780091.

J. Lu, Y. Xin, Z. Zhang, X. Liu, and K. Li. Game-theoretic design of optimal
two-sided rating protocols for service exchange dilemma in crowdsourcing. *IEEE Transactions on Information Forensics and Security*, 13(11):
2801–2815, 2018. doi: 10.1109/TIFS.2018.2834318.

L. Ma, X. Liu, Q. Pei, and Y. Xiang. Privacy-preserving reputation management for edge computing enhanced mobile crowdsensing. *IEEE Transactions on Services Computing*, 12(5):786–799, 2019.

Q. Ma, L. Gao, Y. Liu, and J. Huang. Incentivizing wi-fi network crowdsourcing: A contract theoretic approach. *IEEE/ACM Transactions on Networking*, 26(3):1035–1048, 2018. doi: 10.1109/TNET.2018.2812785.

X. Ma, W. Deng, F. Wang, M. Hu, F. Chen, and M. M. Hassan. Timcc: On data freshness in privacy-preserving incentive mechanism design for continuous crowdsensing using reverse auction. *IEEE Access*, 8:1777–1789, 2020. doi: 10.1109/ACCESS.2019.2962212.

Y. Wang, Y. Li, Z. Chi, and X. Tong. The truthful evolution and incentive for large-scale mobile crowd sensing networks. *IEEE Access*, 6:51187–51199, 2018. doi: 10.1109/ACCESS.2018.2869665.

H. Wu, L. Wang, G. Xue, J. Tang, and D. Yang. Enabling data trustworthiness and user privacy in mobile crowdsensing. *IEEE/ACM Transactions on Networking*, 27(6):2294–2307, 2019. doi: 10.1109/TNET.2019.2944984.

M. Xiao, K. Ma, A. Liu, H. Zhao, Z. Li, K. Zheng, and X. Zhou. Sra: Secure reverse auction for task assignment in spatial crowdsourcing. *IEEE Transactions on Knowledge and Data Engineering*, 32(4):782–796, 2020. doi: 10.1109/TKDE.2019.2893240.

Y. Xing, L. Wang, Z. Li, and Y. Zhan. Multi-attribute crowdsourcing task assignment with stability and satisfactory. *IEEE Access*, 7:133351–133361, 2019. doi: 10.1109/ACCESS.2019.2941045.

J. Xiong, M. Zhao, M. Z. A. Bhuiyan, L. Chen, and Y. Tian. An AI-enabled three-party game framework for guaranteed data privacy in mobile edge crowdsensing of IoT. *IEEE Transactions on Industrial Informatics*, 17(2): 922–933, 2021. doi: 10.1109/TII.2019.2957130.

Qichao Xu, Zhou Su, Shui Yu, and Ying Wang. Trust based incentive scheme to allocate big data tasks with mobile social cloud. *IEEE Transactions on Big Data*, 8(1):113–124, 2022. doi: 10.1109/TBDATA.2017.2764925.

K. Yan, G. Lu, G. Luo, X. Zheng, L. Tian, and A. Maradapu Vera Venkata Sai. Location privacy-aware task bidding and assignment for mobile crowd-sensing. *IEEE Access*, 7:131929–131943, 2019. doi: 10.1109/ACCESS.2019.2940738.

X. Zhang, G. Xue, R. Yu, D. Yang, and J. Tang. Countermeasures against false-name attacks on truthful incentive mechanisms for crowdsourcing. *IEEE Journal on Selected Areas in Communications*, 35(2):478–485, 2017. doi: 10.1109/JSAC.2017.2659229.

Z. Zhang, S. He, J. Chen, and J. Zhang.  Reap: An efficient incentive mechanism for reconciling aggregation accuracy and individual privacy in crowdsensing. *IEEE Transactions on Information Forensics and Security*, 13(12):2995–3007, 2018. doi: 10.1109/TIFS.2018.2834232.

Bowen Zhao, Shaohua Tang, Ximeng Liu, and Xinglin Zhang. Pace: Privacy-preserving and quality-aware incentive mechanism for mobile crowdsensing. *IEEE Transactions on Mobile Computing*, 20(5):1924–1939, 2021. doi: 10.1109/TMC.2020.2973980.

# 7

# Machine Learning Based Privacy/Security Solutions for MCS

After reading this chapter, you should be able to:

- Interpret the role of reinforcement learning in MCS security.
- Compare and contrast problems, solutions, and evaluation metrics for machine learning applications in MCS security.
- Resolve privacy of mobile workers data in machine learning based MCS.

Table 7.1 outlines contemporary approaches in security of machine learning based mobile crowdsourcing. As a defense against fake sensing, provided to the MCS server by selfish workers' smartphones, the server needs to encourage high quality sensing and discourage fake sensing attacks. In this regard, the interactions between the MCS server and MCS workers are modeled as a Stackelberg game. Here, the server is the lead player that determines and broadcasts its payment policy for each sensing accuracy. Each worker is a follower that chooses the sensing effort/accuracy to receive the payment (based on the payment policy) and the sensing accuracy estimated by the server. The conditions to motivate accurate sensing affect the Stackelberg equilibria. Moreover, when the worker sensing models are not known in a dynamic MCS game, deep Q-network reinforcement learning can be used to derive the optimal MCS policy against fake sensing results. To achieve the optimal payment policy, the deep Q-network reinforcement learning is implemented using a convolutional neural network with a high-dimensional state space and action set.

Lack of enough payment and data privacy leakage are two obstacles discouraging workers from participating in crowdsourcing tasks. To motivate workers, each MCS worker may be allowed to submit its sensing data with a specified payment-privacy protection level before the MCS server can

**Table 7.1**    Machine learning for MCS security and privacy.

| Problem | Solution | Evaluation metrics |
|---|---|---|
| Fake sensing results provided to MCS server | Deep Q-network reinforcement learning using convolutional neural networks to learn optimal payment policy | Sensing quality, attack rate, and server utility |
| Incentivizing MCS workers despite lack of system model | Deep reinforcement learning to derive optimal strategies in a payment-privacy protection game | Utility of MCS workers, utility of MCS server, and data aggregation accuracy |
| • Privacy of machine learning training data provided by MCS workers • Attacker reversely inferring training data from the classification model | Differential privacy combined with deep neural networks; injection of noise to the affine transformation of the input data features | Predictive and classification accuracies tested on US census data |
| Location privacy in crowdsourcing intelligent transportation systems | Obfuscation of spatio-temporal data with obfuscation coefficients; requestors use EM algorithm to estimate the task results from the obfuscated uncertain worker locations | Location entropy, crowdsourcing results accuracy |
| Privacy during training for feature learning using crowdsourced big data on the cloud | BGV encryption (homomorphic) to encrypt the private training data on the cloud | Classification accuracy and training efficiency tested on the Animal-20 and NUS-WIDE0-14 datasets |

allocate a corresponding payment to the worker. This is a game for which the Nash equilibrium needs to be derived. Nevertheless, to derive the optimal strategies in this game, it is combined with deep reinforcement learning (Q-learning or deep Q network) to overcome the lack of knowledge about the workers' dynamic payment protection level.

When the crowdsourced data, collected from MCS workers, are fed to machine learning models for classification or prediction purposes, the workers' private data may be exposed in this process. In the mobile crowdsourcing edge computing IoT, i.e., mobile crowdsourcing combined with edge computing, $k$-anonymity algorithm can protect the users' privacy in the random forest classification of crowdsourced data. To achieve differential privacy in deep neural networks, intentional noise is injected to the affine transformation of the input data features. The importance of data features related to target categories is estimated so that less noise is injected to the more important features. To accommodate the heterogeneous feature values, coefficients of injected noise are adaptively selected. BGV, which is a fully homomorphic encryption, is another method for privacy protection of crowdsourced training data on the cloud. Four core operations of BGV include encryption, decryption, secure addition, and secure product. BGV supports the addition and multiplication operations on ciphertexts without bootstrapping.

Spatio-temporal crowdsourced data in intelligent transportation systems exposes locations of workers. Hiding a worker's location negatively affects the quality of spatial crowdsourcing tasks. However, obfuscation arithmetic with appropriate obfuscation coefficients for workers' space and time provides both worker privacy and MCS task quality. Since the location of the worker is uncertain from the viewpoint of the requester, the requester needs to use the machine learning expectation maximization (EM) algorithm to derive the maximum likelihood estimate of the task results from the obfuscated uncertain locations.

## 7.1 Future Research Directions

An area of further exploration is the optimal deep reinforcement learning based payment policies for different applications of crowdsensing, e.g., traffic data aggregation with malicious workers. In addition, noise injection into data features needs to be implemented and tested on various neural network architectures intended for different types of crowdsourced data aggregations. Moreover, novel location obfuscation mechanisms need to be designed against adversaries that launch their attacks based on the probability of workers' locations.

## References

X. Chu, J. Liu, D. Gong, and R. Wang. Preserving location privacy in spatial crowdsourcing under quality control. *IEEE Access*, 7:155851–155859, 2019. doi: 10.1109/ACCESS.2019.2949409.

Y. Liu, H. Wang, M. Peng, J. Guan, J. Xu, and Y. Wang. Deepga: A privacy-preserving data aggregation game in crowdsensing via deep reinforcement learning. *IEEE Internet of Things Journal*, 7(5):4113–4127, 2020. doi: 10.1109/JIOT.2019.2957400.

Y. Wang, M. Gu, J. Ma, and Q. Jin. Dnn-dp: Differential privacy enabled deep neural network learning framework for sensitive crowdsourcing data. *IEEE Transactions on Computational Social Systems*, 7(1):215–224, 2020. doi: 10.1109/TCSS.2019.2950017.

L. Xiao, Y. Li, G. Han, H. Dai, and H. V. Poor. A secure mobile crowdsensing game with deep reinforcement learning. *IEEE Transactions on Information Forensics and Security*, 13(1):35–47, 2018. doi: 10.1109/TIFS.2017.2737968.

J. Xiong, M. Zhao, M. Z. A. Bhuiyan, L. Chen, and Y. Tian. An AI-enabled three-party game framework for guaranteed data privacy in mobile edge crowdsensing of IoT. *IEEE Transactions on Industrial Informatics*, 17(2): 922–933, 2021. doi: 10.1109/TII.2019.2957130.

Q. Zhang, L. T. Yang, Z. Chen, P. Li, and M. J. Deen. Privacy-preserving double-projection deep computation model with crowdsourcing on cloud for big data feature learning. *IEEE Internet of Things Journal*, 5(4):2896–2903, 2018. doi: 10.1109/JIOT.2017.2732735.

# 8

---

# Crowdsourced Mobile Apps

---

After reading this chapter, you should be able to:

- Specify the steps for ciphertext keyword matching between MCS task requestors and workers.
- Apply crowdsourced mechanisms for privacy permission settings upon installing smartphone apps.
- Compare and contrast security of MCS recommendation systems.

## 8.1 Crowdsourced Security for Android Users

Crowdsourcing can be used as a security solution for Android users with untrusted apps that require permission to access users' data. A user with more expertise in an Android user-help-user crowdsourced system can help others by suggesting whether to accept or deny a permission to their data when an Android application requests access to user information. It is challenging, however, to find and expand the network of reliable experts with sufficient level of expertise that will not provide malicious guidance to other users. A solution is to incorporate a rating system (called DroidNet) to identify reliable experts in the network. The reliable experts provide accept/deny permission suggestions to other Android application users. The solution starts by forming a small group of internal trusted experts, called seed experts. Seed experts establish a minimum set of permissions that are necessary for the application functionality. DroidNet expands the network of reliable experts by finding similarities among a common set of permissions by seed experts and other users. These similarities determine the expertise level of each user. The rating of a regular user is iteratively updated by comparing permission suggestions of the user with that of seed experts or other users with a known level of expertise.

### 8.1.1 Crowdsourcing for recommending smartphone app privacy settings

Crowdsourced solicitation of smartphone users' privacy permission settings for various mobile apps leads to a better understanding of users' privacy expectations and allows app-specific unobtrusive privacy recommendations. An example is PriWe, a crowdsourcing-driven system that collects privacy permission settings of the apps installed on smartphones to make proper recommendations to users on how to minimize privacy disclosure upon installing smartphone apps. To encourage smartphone users' participation to share their app permission settings, this task was published and tested on the Amazon Mechanical Turk crowdsourcing platform.

## 8.2 Privacy-preserving MCS Recommendation

Personalized task recommendation mechanisms ensure pushing the matching tasks to potentially interested workers instead of simply publishing tasks without targeting an audience of suitable mobile workers. Recommendations are based on MCS workers' time-varying interests and expertise. However, plaintext exposure of requesters' tasks and workers' interests causes privacy concerns in the presence of an honest but curious MCS platform. Although encryption of tasks and interests preserves privacy, for existing MCS recommendation systems to be effective for ciphertexts, task recommendation needs to be transformed into task access control and keyword-based search. With requesters and workers owning their secret keys, multi-keyword matching can be performed on task requirements and workers' interests represented by multiple keywords.

Keyword search in the ciphertext domain can be conducted using a predefined keyword dictionary. To reduce the computational cost of searching through the keyword dictionary, the vector space model is replaced with a polynomial function to represent task requirements and worker interests as smaller vectors. Multiple keywords, related to task requirements and worker interests, can be expressed using a polynomial function. The steps to perform multiple-keyword matching between multiple requesters and multiple workers include:

1. derive keys based on matrix decomposition and distribute different secret keys to requesters and workers;
2. requestors encrypt task requirements and workers encrypt their interests (with different secret keys by requesters and workers);

**Table 8.1** Recommendation systems for MCS.

| Goal | Approach | Challenges/evaluation |
|---|---|---|
| Avoiding underperforming mobile workers who cause high error rates | Recommendation and ranking mechanisms to generate a list of suitable workers by assigning a topic model to each task and using logistic regression with Bayesian posterior inference to predict topic-specific interest degree/expertise of each MCS worker; Twitter latent Dirichlet allocation method | Time-varying interests of MCS workers; evaluated on multi-tag labeling tasks |
| Private and personalized task recommendation in the ciphertext domain despite a honest but curious MCS cloud server | Requester uses descriptive attributes to specify conditions for the task to be pushed to a worker with matching attributes; multi-authority attribute-based searchable encryption | Computational and time costs of task encryption/decryption |
| Simultaneous task privacy and worker privacy empowered by user accountability and user revocation | Representing task requirements and worker interests as small vectors; key derivation based on matrix decomposition for multi-keyword matching between requesters and workers with proxy re-encryption and asymmetric scalar-product-preserving encryption | Reducing the computational cost associated with predefined keyword dictionary |
| Recommendations to smartphone App users about privacy permission settings | Collaborative filtering to find similar apps and people with similar privacy preferences based on crowdsourced data collection of mobile users' privacy permission settings; seeking users' feedback to improve the accuracy of recommendations | Evaluated on hundreds of participants on Amazon Mechanical Turks for several days and on Android SDK (PriWe App) |

**Table 8.1**  *Continued.*

| Goal | Approach | Challenges/evaluation |
|---|---|---|
| Fairness in mobile worker recruitment by inducing uniform probability of selection | Determining the membership function of each worker attribute and using fuzzy comprehensive evaluation to calculate the value of each attribute; secure multi-party sorting based on fuzzy closeness with mobile participants using homomorphism of semantic security encryption | Data quality variations caused by dynamically varying task requirements; computation /communication overhead; cosine similarity index calculation time; task budget consumption ratio |
| Collusion between MCS server and participants to reveal private information during recruitment | Secret sharing during mobile worker recruitment using an increasing submodular function as the computation function of the sensing quality | NP-hardness; achieving logarithmic approximation ratio (through submodular sensing quality function) |

3. securely compute the inner products between the encrypted task requirements and workers' interests using asymmetric scalar-product-preserving encryption together with proxy re-encryption.

This scheme allows for user revocation.

Another enabler to construct a privacy-preserving personalized recommendation system is combining multi-authority attribute-based encryption and searchable encryption schemes. More specifically, instead of relying on a single authority to issue public and private keys, every requester becomes an authority to encrypt their own tasks' attributes and issue keys for authorized workers according to the workers' interest or expertise attributes. Table 8.1 explores various privacy goals, approaches, and challenges in MCS recommendation systems.

To prevent astroturfing, which negatively affects task quality and wastes resources, a topic is assigned to each task by a fine-grained recommendation mechanism through interest-expertise collaborative awareness. After estimating the topic-specific expertise level and interest degree of workers by using historical task records, the recommendation system comes up with a list of suitable workers for topic-specific tasks.

## 8.3 Privacy-preserving Mobile Worker Recruitment

During worker recruitment, the reward requested by a mobile worker reveals private information such as the tasks that the worker can perform, the sensing quality, etc. The tasks a user can perform may expose users' visited sites while the sensing quality exposes the visits' frequency, time, geographical distance, etc. Additionally, the workers' sensed data must be kept private from other competing workers. Randomness methods, such as differential privacy, are not accurate for the crowdsensing tasks that require precision. Despite being a countermeasure, homomorphic encryption and garbled circuit protocols impose expensive computation/communication overhead on mobile devices. To tackle these issues, secret sharing is combined with greedy prioritization of workers with the best total sensing qualities of all tasks (compared to a quality threshold) to recruit optimal workers.

To identify matching mobile workers, cosine similarity scores calculate the similarity between the vector of task attributes and the worker's capability/interest vector. To ensure both fairness and privacy in worker recruitment, the fuzzy comprehensive evaluation and fuzzy closeness are used along with secure multi-party worker sorting. More specifically, to sort the matching workers with secret inputs, homomorphism of semantic security encryption is used to calculate the fuzzy closeness.

## 8.4 Future Research Directions

It is essential to design lightweight secure protocols, which do not depend on cryptography or a trusted third party. This can be done by improving the computational efficiency of worker recruitment to adapt to dynamically varying task requirements; coming up with more measurable privacy leakage metrics for worker recruitment; handling task recommendations that involve a group of MCS participants rather than a single user (i.e., larger-scale MCS systems); and deploying big datasets and numerous app store applications.

## References

Z. Guo, C. Tang, W. Niu, Y. Fu, T. Wu, H. Xia, and H. Tang. Fine-grained recommendation mechanism to curb astroturfing in crowdsourcing systems. *IEEE Access*, 5:15529–15541, 2017. doi: 10.1109/ACCESS.2017.2731360.

T. Li, T. Jung, Z. Qiu, H. Li, L. Cao, and Y. Wang. Scalable privacy-preserving participant selection for mobile crowdsensing systems: Participant grouping and secure group bidding. *IEEE Transactions on Network Science and Engineering*, 7(2):855–868, 2020. doi: 10.1109/TNSE.2018.2791948.

R. Liu, J. Cao, K. Zhang, W. Gao, J. Liang, and L. Yang. When privacy meets usability: Unobtrusive privacy permission recommendation system for mobile apps based on crowdsourcing. *IEEE Transactions on Services Computing*, 11(5):864–878, 2018. doi: 10.1109/TSC.2016.2605089.

R. Liu, J. Liang, J. Cao, K. Zhang, W. Gao, L. Yang, and R. Yu. Understanding mobile users' privacy expectations: A recommendation-based method through crowdsourcing. *IEEE Transactions on Services Computing*, 12(2): 304–318, 2019. doi: 10.1109/TSC.2016.2636285.

B. Rashidi, C. Fung, A. Nguyen, T. Vu, and E. Bertino. Android user privacy preserving through crowdsourcing. *IEEE Transactions on Information Forensics and Security*, 13(3):773–787, 2018.

J. Shu, X. Jia, K. Yang, and H. Wang. Privacy-preserving task recommendation services for crowdsourcing. *IEEE Transactions on Services Computing*, 14(1):235–247, 2021. doi: 10.1109/TSC.2018.2791601.

M. Xiao, G. Gao, J. Wu, S. Zhang, and L. Huang. Privacy-preserving user recruitment protocol for mobile crowdsensing. *IEEE/ACM Transactions on Networking*, 28(2):519–532, 2020. doi: 10.1109/TNET.2019.2962362.

J. Xiong, X. Chen, Q. Yang, L. Chen, and Z. Yao. A task-oriented user selection incentive mechanism in edge-aided mobile crowdsensing. *IEEE Transactions on Network Science and Engineering*, 7(4):2347–2360, 2020. doi: 10.1109/TNSE.2019.2940958.

H. Yin, Y. Xiong, T. Deng, H. Deng, and P. Zhu. A privacy-preserving and identity-based personalized recommendation scheme for encrypted tasks in crowdsourcing. *IEEE Access*, 7:138857–138871, 2019. doi: 10.1109/ACCESS.2019.2943114.

# 9

# Reliable Industrial IoT using Crowdsourcing

After reading this chapter, you should be able to:

- Identify elements of crowdsourced industrial IoT protection.
- State the main components of data authentication in the cloud.
- Determine methods to reduce computational cost of crowdsourced industrial IoT data verification.
- Compare and contrast approaches and evaluation metrics for industrial IoT security.

MCS enables industrial and e-healthcare services through industrial IoT (IIoT). Figure 9.1 and Table 9.1 summarize the elements and solutions for the protection of crowdsourced industrial IoT. A major goal in battery-limited MCS-based IIoT is to avoid computationally expensive schemes, such as elliptic curve point multiplication or modular exponentiation operation. To this end, lightweight chaotic-map-based multifactor user authentication (i.e., smart card, password, biometrics, etc.) allows remote access or storage of medical data to authorized users (e.g., healthcare personnel or patients in e-healthcare crowdsourced IoT).

Another security issue in MCS-based IIoT arises from outsourcing the data to the cloud to reduce the costs of data management, sharing, and computation. For data authentication in the cloud, without the need for a key-escrow, certificateless signature (CLS) can be used as an identity–based signature technique. Nevertheless, the computational cost of cryptographic operations along with the probabilistic nature of map-to-point hash function and random oracle model render the CLS scheme impractical for IIoT due to device storage and bandwidth constraints. Instead, bilinear pairing identity based signcryption circumvents the need for map-to-point hash function and random oracle model and enables both authentication and confidentiality of crowdsourced data under limited storage and low-bandwidth IIoT conditions.

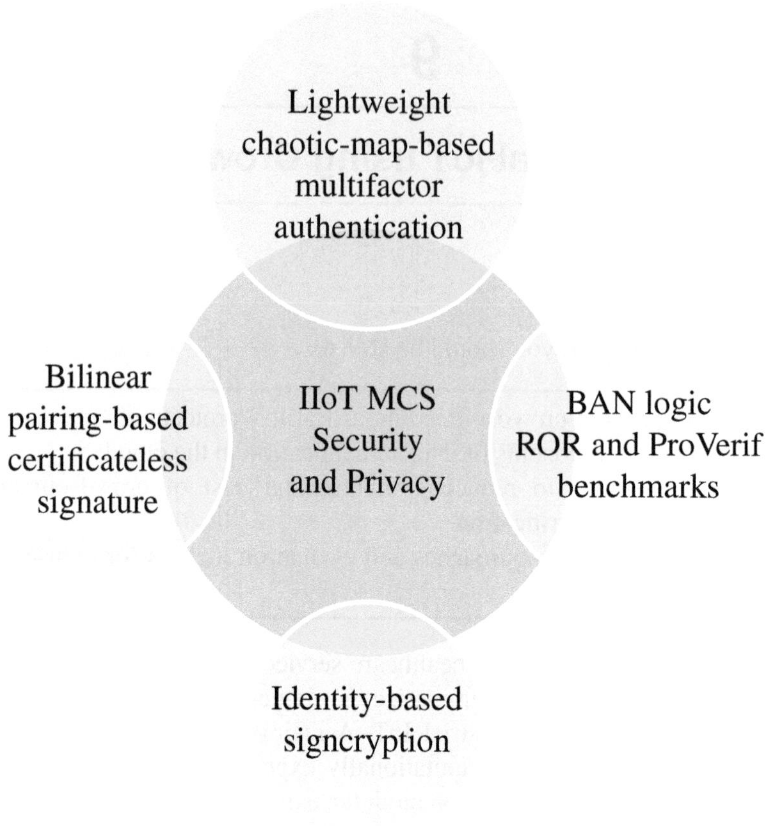

Lightweight
chaotic-map-based
multifactor
authentication

Bilinear
pairing-based
certificateless
signature

IIoT MCS
Security
and Privacy

BAN logic
ROR and ProVerif
benchmarks

Identity-based
signcryption

**Figure 9.1**  Elements of crowdsourced IIoT protection.

The computational cost of authenticated IIoT data creation and verification can be further reduced by discarding the pairing computation. Common benchmarks to verify the security of remote authentication schemes in MCS IIoT include: real-or-random (ROR) model (for the verification of key security) and Burrows–Abadi–Needham (BAN) logic (for the verification of the security of mutual authentication between a user and the MCS server).

## 9.1 Future Research Directions

Research directions for lightweight CLS methods on low-power MCS IIoT devices include:

**Table 9.1**  MCS industrial IoT privacy and security.

| Problem | Approach | Challenges/evaluation metrics |
| --- | --- | --- |
| Data authenticity and untrustworthiness of third parties in cloud-assisted IIoT | Bilinear pairing-based certificateless signature without map-to-point hash function and random oracle model | Communication bandwidth and IoT device storage constraints |
| Signature forgery attacks, public key replacement attacks, and malicious passive third parties | Elliptic curve partial private key generation into the short certificateless signature scheme and key exchange in the partial private key generation to enable crowdsourced IIoT communication over public channels | Robustness against chosen-message attacks; computation and storage |
| Personalized privacy measurement in MCS IIoT with utility maximization for MCS participants | Combination of game theoretical rational uploading strategies and encryption | Balance between task quality and privacy; real-time data confidentiality and integrity |
| Impersonation attack by obtaining the server's master key | Direct authentication of the user by the server, using the authentication factor instead of the server authenticating the secret key stored at the user's mobile device; all authentication factors (e.g., biometrics, password, etc.) acting as a part of the secret key and participating in the authentication and key agreement | Time consumption on 5G/6G IoT devices; smaller key size |
| Lightweight remote user authentication in e-healthcare IoT | Multifactor authentication based on extended chaotic maps verified on ProVerif verification tool; verification of key security, using the real-or-random (ROR) model and verification of the security of mutual authentication between a user and the medical server using Burrows–Abadi–Needham (BAN) logic | Low communication and computational overhead for battery-limited healthcare devices |

1. further reduction of the pairing overhead of bilinear pairing for sign-crypted IIoT;
2. design of identity-based CLS schemes with revocation capability;
3. extension of existing authentication schemes for cloud-assisted MCS IIoT to multi-server environments.

## References

A. Karati, S. H. Islam, G. P. Biswas, M. Z. A. Bhuiyan, P. Vijayaku-mar, and M. Karuppiah. Provably secure identity-based signcryp-tion scheme for crowdsourced industrial internet of things environ-ments. *IEEE Internet of Things Journal*, 5(4):2904–2914, 2018a. doi: 10.1109/JIOT.2017.2741580.

A. Karati, S. H. Islam, and M. Karuppiah. Provably secure and lightweight certificateless signature scheme for IIoT environments. *IEEE Transactions on Industrial Informatics*, 14(8):3701–3711, 2018b. doi: 10.1109/TII.2018.2794991.

W. Liu, X. Wang, and W. Peng. Secure remote multi-factor authenti-cation scheme based on chaotic map zero-knowledge proof for crowd-sourcing internet of things. *IEEE Access*, 8:8754–8767, 2020. doi: 10.1109/ACCESS.2019.2962912.

S. Roy, S. Chatterjee, A. K. Das, S. Chattopadhyay, S. Kumari, and M. Jo. Chaotic map-based anonymous user authentication scheme with user biometrics and fuzzy extractor for crowdsourcing internet of things. *IEEE Internet of Things Journal*, 5(4):2884–2895, 2018. doi: 10.1109/JIOT.2017.2714179.

Shabnam Sodagari. Trends for mobile iot crowdsourcing privacy and security in the big data era. *IEEE Transactions on Technology and Society*, 3 (3):199–225, 2022. doi: 10.1109/TTS.2022.3191515. ©[2022]IEEE. Reprinted, with permission.

J. Xiong, R. Ma, L. Chen, Y. Tian, Q. Li, X. Liu, and Z. Yao. A per-sonalized privacy protection framework for mobile crowdsensing in IIoT. *IEEE Transactions on Industrial Informatics*, 16(6):4231–4241, 2020. doi: 10.1109/TII.2019.2948068.

Y. Zhang, R. H. Deng, D. Zheng, J. Li, P. Wu, and J. Cao. Efficient and robust certificateless signature for data crowdsensing in cloud-assisted industrial IoT. *IEEE Transactions on Industrial Informatics*, 15(9):5099–5108, 2019. doi: 10.1109/TII.2019.2894108.

# 10

## Misinformation, Fake News, and Crowdsourcing

After reading this chapter, you should be able to:

- Utilize crowdsourcing against misinformation.
- Develop social MCS security.
- Establish truth discovery in MCS systems.

## 10.1 Truth Discovery Against Data Falsification in MCS

Some MCS platforms pursue monetization of knowledge and, hence, need truth discovery to mine the knowledge, from unreliable sensing data. Truth discovery ensures fair monetization by estimating user reliability degrees and by inferring truthful information via reliability-aware data aggregation. However, private information of MCS participants (identity, workers' locations, investment of the task requestor, etc.) may be exposed during truth discovery process. One solution is to conduct truth discovery in the encrypted domain in the cloud using lightweight additively homomorphic encryption and garbled circuits. The encrypted extracted truth is then sent to the requester for decryption. Nevertheless, the iterative transmission of large homomorphic ciphertexts for dynamic users imposes extra costs of computation, bandwidth, fault tolerance, and group management. The process of truth discovery involves a weighted collection of crowdsensed reports to give more weights to more reliable workers. Random masking applied to weighted data aggregation prevents the leakage of individual sensory data or users' weights in iterative truth discovery. Table 10.1 highlights MCS truth discovery schemes to hinder data falsification.

Due to proximity of fog nodes to mobile MCS users, they can perform real-time truth discovery with low latency and lower bandwidth. Closeness

**Table 10.1**   Overview of truth discovery against data falsification in MCS.

| Goal | Approach | Implementation |
|---|---|---|
| Privacy of the sensing values and weights (reliability degrees) of MCS users, as well as the requester's inferred truth | • Two non-colluding independent cloud servers (one bridging the workers and requesters and the other discovering truth in the encrypted domain) perform truth discovery in encrypted domain before sending to the requestor for decryption<br>• Lightweight additively homomorphic encryption and garbled circuits | Crowdsourced indoor floorplan reconstruction on Microsoft Azure (MCS requester and cloud server) using D12 instance (4 cores, 28-GB RAM, Ubuntu Server 16.04 LTS system), and Samsung Galaxy S4 Android phone (MCS worker), four-core 1.6 GHz processor, four-core 1.2 GHz processor, and 2.0 GB RAM; ObliVM-lang2 for garbled circuits |
| Reducing communication bandwidth and computation in privacy-preserving large-scale iterative MCS truth discovery | Splitting-based encryption combined with homomorphic encryption in a two-server model with random masking applied on weighted data aggregation | Execution time and convergence measured on Amazon EC2 c4.4xlarge instance (as the server) with Xeon E5-2666 processor with 16× 2.9 GHz vCPU, 30 GB memory and Samsung Galaxy S6 Android phone (as the user) |
| Discouraging untruthful reports while the identities/locations of MCS workers are cloaked for privacy | • Penalization mechanism design to enforce truthfulness as the optimal strategy<br>• Rewarding higher profits to encourage calibration of intrinsic sensing biases | Accuracy of crowdsensed outdoor temperature data reported by taxis in Rome on OMNeT++ 4.6 |
| Privacy for highly mobile (e.g., vehicular) crowdsensing despite untrustworthy fog nodes involved in MCS truth discovery | • Outsourcing truth estimation to both the cloud and fog nodes<br>• Super-increasing sequence to integrate multidimensional weighted data, instead of direct encryption and upload<br>• Perturbation, hash chain, and homomorphic Paillier encryption to shift all user workload to the MCS server | Computational costs and communication, runtime, and accuracy of truth discovery on a testbed with Android phones (mobile users) with 1.5 GHz and 2-GB RAM, and a laptop with 2.5 GHz Intel Core i7 and 16-GB RAM (as fog and cloud) |

to mobile users allows fog nodes to authenticate MCS participants to prevent false data injection attack. Nevertheless, if fog nodes are not trusted, countermeasures include perturbation, homomorphic Paillier encryption, one-way hash chain, and super-increasing sequence techniques to outsource truth estimation to the cloud.

Since privacy-preserving methods may sometimes protect the identities of malicious users, they can contradict truth discovery and data quality. Enriching truth discovery with game theory and algorithmic mechanism design, via incentive and penalty policies, motivates truthful sensing results while preserving privacy.

## 10.2  Social MCS Privacy

The popularity and openness of crowdsourced data from mobile users in social networks and social IoT may jeopardize mobile users' privacy. It provides individuals with an opportunity to exhibit antisocial behavior (e.g., free riding) to decrease the social welfare. Game theoretical mechanisms, such as pricing/reward and reputation/rating, to tag the mobile participants' social status, can incentivize compliance with social norms. Table 10.2 explores different security problems, approaches, and challenges in the context of social crowdsourcing.

Online aggregate monitoring over infinite streams combined with differential privacy enables real-time spatio-temporal data publishing in social networks, where population statistics are continuously published. The privacy of statistics published on infinite time stamps are provided through adaptive sampling, adaptive budget allocation, dynamic grouping, perturbation, and filtering. To improve the utility of released data, i.e., to minimize the total group error, deep learning may be used to predict the statistics of spatial regions.

Reporting local histograms, instead of raw data, can prevent the privacy leakage caused by participants' social coupling, measured through their data correlation. Gaussian Markov random fields model the correlations underlying the participants' data. The interaction of the MCS server and participants leans itself to a Stackelberg game, where the server chooses its reward policy and participants choose their noise levels relevant to their social correlation. The policies depend on the relationship between MCS participants' Nash equilibria, the payment mechanism, budget, and the required task accuracy. Malicious users may report falsified noise levels to gain higher payment.

**Table 10.2**    Trustworthy social MCS systems.

| Problem | Approach | Challenges |
|---|---|---|
| Antisocial behavior (e.g., free riding) to decrease the MCS social welfare | Socially optimal rating protocol based on game theory through an incentive mechanism by integrating the pricing and social status reputation | Quantifying social norm and compliance |
| Real-time spatio-temporal data publishing in crowdsourced social networks with privacy preservation | Integration of adaptive sampling, adaptive budget allocation, dynamic grouping, perturbation, and filtering for privacy-preserving statistics publishing | The utility of data publishing |
| Privacy leakage through correlation attacks caused by social relationships of MCS participants | Socially private correlated local histograms with MCS participants adding noise to protect their privacy; Stackelberg game modeling of interactions between the MCS server and participants | Falsified noise levels chosen by MCS participants to achieve higher payoffs |
| Privacy of task requesters in social IoT revealed by friendship/collaboration among MCS workers in routing of tasks among multihop friends | Multihop routing incentive mechanism to motivate workers to forward tasks to their expert friends | Utility maximization under privacy and budget feasibility constraints; tradeoff between privacy and task accuracy; approximation ratio of task assignment algorithm |
| Sybil-proof social MCS | Reverse auction incentives to recruit workers based on their social neighbors and not fictitious identities | Social cost; running time; MCS users' utilities |

Payment mechanisms that assert truthfulness as a dominant strategy can thwart false reporting.

In social IoT, the couplings among MCS workers are useful for worker recruitment to perform collaborative multihop tasks. Incentive mechanisms protect the requestors' privacy in multihop routing tasks, taking into account the utility budget constraints. For example, consider a spatial MCS in which workers compete to perform multiple tasks by taking detours from their original travel paths. The task assignment must maximize the social welfare of MCS participants and protect workers' privacy. To evaluate trustworthiness of participants, their social trust degrees are updated based on their social ties and the importance of allocated tasks. The reputation update is based on social norm. Social norms consist of a social strategy and a reputation scheme to regulate the behavior of participants. Social norms are designed to punish deviations from the selected social strategy.

## 10.3 Misinformation Thwarted by Crowdsourcing

Rumors, fake news, or misinformation can cause serious problems, especially following disasters, when users do not have enough time for verifying the credibility of online posts. Methods for truth discovery and social MCS, discussed previously, can be used to detect misinformation. Other major fake news detection strategies include content analysis, social context (e.g., diffusion patterns), and machine learning classification/prediction.

Seeking feedback from MCS mobile workers about the classification of news (fake or true) is less expensive, compared with professional journalists or subject experts. However, it could be less reliable than the opinion of experts. To strike a balance for this tradeoff, a crowd knowledge graph is constructed by combining the feedback from experts and non-expert MCS workers about misinformation. The crowdsourced judgments can then be combined with machine learning to predict their accuracy. For example, to detect COVID-19 misinformation, natural language processing (NLP) was used to extract key information in the news content. MCS workers were tasked with reading the content to extract the key knowledge related to the NLP outputs.

Moreover, the immutability and transparency of crowdsourced news (e.g., Twitter feeds) stored on the blockchain enable fake news detection. Specifically, machine learning continuously learns from the output of the PoS smart contract, while validators from the public (Ethereum) blockchain are incentivized with rewards for contributing reliable information. The machine learning classifier acts as one of the validators in the PoS consensus. The final verdict from the smart contract, about the truth of the news, enriches the training dataset to dynamically improve the machine learning classification outputs.

Leveraging the differences of diffusion patterns between misinformation and true information, Bayesian logistic regression can infer the credibility of a message by observing the latent attributes of the message, the users interacting with it, and their reactions to the message. To this end, example available datasets include:

- CREDBANK (set of Twitter conversations about events and corresponding crowdsourced accuracy assessments for each event);
- PHEME (curated dataset of conversation threads about Twitter rumors and journalists' annotation assessments of their truthfulness);
- BuzzFeed dataset of highly shared true and false political stories.

Figure 10.1 summarizes the MCS-based approach to fake news and misinformation discovery.

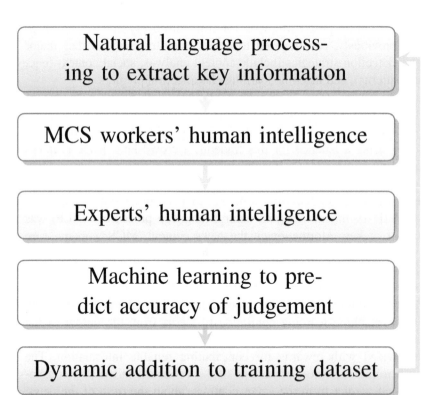

**Figure 10.1**   MCS-based approach against misinformation and fake news.

### 10.3.1 Future research directions

Exploring various types of weight functions in weighted data aggregation for truth discovery (e.g., weight functions that are based on linear operations between a user's distance and the summation of distances across all users) has the potential to improve MCS truth discovery. Areas of further research include:

- generalizing the schemes to maximize a participant's average revenue from all tasks instead of just the expected one-period utility;
- designing competition games for temporary social IoT users instead of permanent users;
- studying security vulnerabilities of MCS social IoT to various types of tasks (other than labeling);
- lightweight edge-based design against sybil attacks in large-scale social IoT MCS networks;
- extension of the existing MCS models to news topics with mixed content;
- estimation of the partial truthfulness of information;
- classification algorithms for news with true content but misleading headlines;
- advancing the integration of artificial intelligence with crowdsourced detection and estimation tasks;
- faster news interpretation and discovery methods.

## References

Cody Buntain and Jennifer Golbeck. Automatically identifying fake news in popular Twitter threads. In *IEEE International Conference on Smart Cloud (SmartCloud)*, pages 208–215, 2017.

Chengjun Cai, Yifeng Zheng, Anxin Zhou, and Cong Wang. Building a secure knowledge marketplace over crowdsensed data streams. *IEEE Transactions on Dependable and Secure Computing*, 18(6):2601–2616, 2021. doi: 10.1109/TDSC.2019.2958901.

Marco L. Della Vedova, Eugenio Tacchini, Stefano Moret, Gabriele Ballarin, Massimo DiPierro, and Luca de Alfaro. Automatic online fake news detection combining content and social signals. In *22nd Conference of Open Innovations Association (FRUCT)*, pages 272–279, 2018.

X. Gan, Y. Li, Y. Huang, L. Fu, and X. Wang.   When crowdsourcing meets social iot: An efficient privacy-preserving incentive mechanism. *IEEE Internet of Things Journal*, 6(6):9707–9721, 2019.   doi: 10.1109/JIOT.2019.2930659.

L. Jiang, X. Niu, J. Xu, Y. Wang, Y. Wu, and L. Xu.   Time-sensitive and sybil-proof incentive mechanisms for mobile crowdsensing via social network. *IEEE Access*, 6:48156–48168, 2018.   doi: 10.1109/ACCESS.2018.2868180.

Ziyi Kou, Lanyu Shang, Yang Zhang, Christina Youn, and Dong Wang. Fakesens: A social sensing approach to covid-19 misinformation detection on social media. In *17th International Conference on Distributed Computing in Sensor Systems (DCOSS)*, pages 140–147, 2021.

J. Lu, C. Tang, X. Li, and Q. Wu.   Designing socially-optimal rating protocols for crowdsourcing contest dilemma. *IEEE Transactions on Information Forensics and Security*, 12(6):1330–1344, 2017.   doi: 10.1109/TIFS.2017.2656468.

Abiola Osho, Caden Waters, and George Amariucai.   An implicit crowdsourcing approach to rumor identification in online social networks.   In *IEEE/ACM International Conference on Advances in Social Networks Analysis and Mining (ASONAM)*, pages 174–182, 2020.

Q. Wang, Y. Zhang, X. Lu, Z. Wang, Z. Qin, and K. Ren.   Real-time and spatio-temporal crowd-sourced social network data publishing with differential privacy. *IEEE Transactions on Dependable and Secure Computing*, 15(4):591–606, 2018. doi: 10.1109/TDSC.2016.2599873.

M. Xiao, K. Ma, A. Liu, H. Zhao, Z. Li, K. Zheng, and X. Zhou.   Sra: Secure reverse auction for task assignment in spatial crowdsourcing. *IEEE Transactions on Knowledge and Data Engineering*, 32(4):782–796, 2020. doi: 10.1109/TKDE.2019.2893240.

G. Yang, Z. Shi, S. He, and J. Zhang.   Socially privacy-preserving data collection for crowdsensing. *IEEE Transactions on Vehicular Technology*, 69(1):851–861, 2020. doi: 10.1109/TVT.2019.2950907.

Tan Hui Yang Zen, Chin Bing Hong, Purnima Murali Mohan, and Vivek Balachandran.   ABC-Verify: AI-Blockchain integrated framework for tweet misinformation detection. In *IEEE International Conference on Service Operations and Logistics, and Informatics (SOLI)*, pages 1–5, 2021.

C. Zhang, L. Zhu, C. Xu, X. Liu, and K. Sharif.   Reliable and privacy-preserving truth discovery for mobile crowdsensing systems. *IEEE Transactions on Dependable and Secure Computing*, 18(3):1245–1260, 2021. doi: 10.1109/TDSC.2019.2919517.

Y. Zhang and M. van der Schaar. Reputation-based incentive protocols in crowdsourcing applications. In *2012 Proceedings IEEE INFOCOM*, pages 2140–2148, 2012.

C. Zhao, S. Yang, and J. A. McCann. On the data quality in privacy-preserving mobile crowdsensing systems with untruthful reporting. *IEEE Transactions on Mobile Computing*, 20(2):647–661, 2021. doi: 10.1109/TMC.2019.2943468.

Y. Zheng, H. Duan, and C. Wang. Learning the truth privately and confidently: Encrypted confidence-aware truth discovery in mobile crowdsensing. *IEEE Transactions on Information Forensics and Security*, 13(10): 2475–2489, 2018. doi: 10.1109/TIFS.2018.2819134.

Y. Zheng, H. Duan, X. Yuan, and C. Wang. Privacy-aware and efficient mobile crowdsensing with truth discovery. *IEEE Transactions on Dependable and Secure Computing*, 17(1):121–133, 2020. doi: 10.1109/TDSC.2017.2753245.

# 11

# Security in 6G and Wi-Fi Communications Leveraging Mobile Crowdsensing

After reading this chapter, you should be able to:

- Distinguish attacks on crowdsensed wireless systems.
- Categorize strategies for securing crowdsensed wireless systems.
- Improve trust in crowdsensed Wi-Fi sharing.

Some crowdsensing applications (e.g., OpenSignal, etc.) measure the true state of the wireless carrier coverage to find hotspots. Mobile crowdsensing measurements can be used to update real-time databases of spectrum white spaces for dynamic spectrum sharing (DSS). This gives rise to several issues, such as

- spectrum misuse by some secondary users;
- location privacy of crowdsensing mobile devices;
- outlier sensing results.

The use of mobile crowdsensing in wireless systems is not limited to spectrum sensing in search of white spaces, but also the numerous cellular user equipments (UEs), e.g., mobile phones, can measure various communication parameters, e.g., signal to interference plus noise ratio (SINR), throughput, delay, etc. Nevertheless, there is little knowledge and control on the timing, locations (e.g., indoor and outdoor), or the cell load conditions under which the ubiquitous mobile UEs perform their measurements.

## 11.1 Untrusted Spectrum Service Provider

The spectrum service provider needs to know the location of mobile users to assign them a spectrum sensing task. Nevertheless, locations of mobile nodes that participate in the spectrum sensing task need to be protected from

**Table 11.1**    Security and privacy for MCS-based 6G communications.

| Problem | Approach |
|---|---|
| Spectrum misuse detection | Mobile crowdsensing workers authenticate secondary user by verifying and decoding spectrum permits embedded in physical-layer signals. |
| Trust and transparency in collaborative D2D MCS spectrum sensing against passive eavesdropping, impersonating, man-in-the-middle, trust forging, collusion, and independent negative attacks | • Shared secret key for device pairing in the initial encounter<br>• Updating the trustworthiness of a device using Gompertz function reputation mapping based on history of transmission delay, data rate, packet loss, etc. |
| Location privacy of mobile workers in crowdsourced spectrum sensing | • Location-based $k$-anonymity mobile grouping<br>• Differential privacy with the objective of minimum social cost |
| Incentives to encourage accuracy in crowdsourced spectrum sensing for white spaces (or received signal strength fingerprinting), while minimizing requestors' payment | Monetary and social motivation via truthful reverse auction-based winning group selection, considering individual rationality and energy consumption by associating each sensor's true spectrum sensing cost to its current location |

an untrusted spectrum service provider. To this end, the dynamic spectrum sharing crowdsensing needs a trusted cellular service provider (CSP) that is a reliable third party between sensing mobile nodes and the spectrum service provider. CSP uses differential privacy by spatial decomposition of collected mobile locations. CSP partitions the area into regions and adds noise to users' location data points in each region. Only after adding noise, the CSP shares the results with the spectrum service provider.

$k$-anonymity grouping enables each UE in MCS spectrum sensing to hide its private information (e.g., location) from an untrusted spectrum database administrator. Here, the sensing results of the whole group of $k$ UEs are collectively reported, as opposed to individual reporting.

## 11.2  Untrusted Spectrum Sensing UEs

Even with a fully trusted spectrum database administrator, the participating UEs in the sensing task may be curious to infer the private information of each other. In the $k$-anonymity grouping mentioned above, there may be some malicious UEs among the group. As a countermeasure, each UE needs a grouping rule to ensure joining a reliable group of UEs. For example, a sensing UE can form groups within its social network or location proximity. Moreover, the desire for gaining more payment may prevent some UEs from revealing their true cost of spectrum sensing to the database administrator. Reverse auction is a truthful incentive mechanism to ensure that no UE in the MCS spectrum sensing obtains profit by reporting a higher cost.

After UEs register with the database administrator, each UE will be given a unique pseudonym, shared with other UEs. To show unbiased selection, the spectrum service provider announces the spectrum-sensing auction results by using the unique pseudonym of winning UEs. If the cost of task performance is revealed, curious UEs may be able to infer private information of other UEs by observing the changes in the auction results, e.g., if the cost is related to parameters, such as the spatial distance between UEs locations and the sensing task. This is especially important when task collaboration among spectrum sensing UEs in a crowdsensed database is enabled by device-to-device (D2D) communication. D2D pairing needs to be established in a secure, autonomous, transparent, and fast manner. To this end, the trustworthiness of participating devices needs to be estimated in real time to enable each device to establish a secure connection with the most trustworthy neighboring device.

Once UEs register with the base station (database administrator or spectrum service provider), to obtain a verifiable pseudonym, their trust value will be updated after each D2D pairing, based on their performance history.

There are several ways for attackers to compromise D2D pairing:

1. Attacks targeting the connection phase:

   - eavesdropping of the D2D communication between two legitimate UEs by a third-party UE;
   - impersonation of a legitimate UE's credentials to fool other UEs toward establishing connection;
   - an adversary may come in the middle of two legitimate UEs, without being noticed. In the man-in-the-middle attack, the two legitimate UEs mistakenly think they are connecting to each other, whereas their connection is actually via the adversary;
   - a UE forges its trust value to mislead other UEs about its trustworthiness;

- a malicious UE always or sometimes rates its connection experience with trustworthy UEs as a negative one, to undermine other UEs' trust value;
- collusive attack in which a subset of malicious UEs rate each other to be trusted, while they rate other UEs outside their collusion to be untrusted.

2. Attacks on the traffic (e.g., false data injection), after the connection is established.

Some countermeasures require any two of registered D2D UEs to negotiate a shared key. The process involves certificateless public key cryptography for a unique private–public key pair for each registered UE. The base station (spectrum database administrator or service provider) will not be able to restore such shared keys, owing to a private share exclusively being held by the UE only.

The spectrum service provider can use reverse auctions for sensor selection with the goal of running truthful crowdsourcing to minimize its payment. Even if the claimed cost (tied to distance) of each participant is hidden, still some location proximity information of devices may be inferred when winners for various published tasks at different rounds of reverse auction are revealed. In MCS applications where each sensor's true cost for spectrum sensing is related to its location, differential location privacy is a viable solution.

## 11.3 Spectrum Permit Verification by Crowdsensing

To prevent spectrum misuse in DSS through secondary user authentication, the transmitter is required to embed a spectrum permit into its physical-layer signals, which can be decoded and verified by ubiquitous crowdsensing mobile users. The spectrum permit could be embedded in various ways, including the modification of original constellation points to higher and lower power levels, or a higher-order constellation than the original one at the same transmission-power level.

## 11.4 Trust in MCS-based Wi-Fi Sharing

Crowdsourcing is an economic way to enlarge the Wi-Fi coverage area by allowing individual owners of private home Wi-Fi access points to share their Wi-Fi access points with each other. For example, Fon is an example of a shared Wi-Fi network with millions of Wi-Fi spots around the world. To resolve the issue of trust among unfamiliar access point owners, contracts that are designed by network operators incentivize Wi-Fi crowdsourcing. However, contracts face the challenge of incomplete information emerging from private mobility patterns and private Wi-Fi access quality of owners. Thus, the contract needs to elicit truthful information from users, via pricing and revenue incentives, to maximize the network operator's profit. More specifically, each contract item has a Wi-Fi access price and a subscription fee. The access price is the amount that each user can charge other users who use its access point. The subscription fee is the amount that a user needs to pay the operator for joining the network of crowdsourced Wi-Fi. However, the choices of each user are tightly coupled to its privacy and the choices of other users. Game theory models help the network operator with pricing and revenue contract design by finding the equilibrium choices of all users.

Received signal strength (RSS) fingerprinting can be done by crowd-sensed data collection. Truthful auction-based incentive mechanisms improve the quality of the collected fingerprints, based on a quality metric that characterizes the joint impact of privacy and spatial coverage. The design of the individually rational auction-based incentive must account for the limited budget of the MCS server and the fact that workers may misreport their costs to gain profit. Table 11.1 summarizes approaches toward security and privacy in MCS-based wireless systems.

## 11.5 Future Research Directions

- Privacy provisioning for mobile participants in the MCS-based wireless sensing may negatively affect the accuracy of results. Addressing this tradeoff is a future research direction.
- The spectrum white space sensing needs to be done in real time, due to rapidly changing wireless radio environments. Therefore, the roles of temporal factors in any secure and private crowdsensed spectrum searching task allocation and integration of this application of MCS with edge computing and/or the cloud need further investigation.
- Extension of the crowdsourced Wi-Fi communities with a single operator to multiple competing network operators, to serve heterogeneous Wi-Fi users with varying traffic demands and mobility patterns, is an area of further exploration.

## References

Z. Huang and Y. Gong. Differential location privacy for crowdsourced spectrum sensing. In *2017 IEEE Conference on Communications and Network Security (CNS)*, pages 1–9, 2017.

X. Jin and Y. Zhang. Privacy-preserving crowdsourced spectrum sensing. *IEEE/ACM Transactions on Networking*, 26(3):1236–1249, 2018. doi: 10.1109/TNET.2018.2823272.

X. Jin, J. Sun, R. Zhang, Y. Zhang, and C. Zhang. Specguard: Spectrum misuse detection in dynamic spectrum access systems. *IEEE Transactions on Mobile Computing*, 17(12):2925–2938, 2018. doi: 10.1109/TMC.2018.2823314.

W. Li, C. Zhang, and Y. Tanaka. Privacy-aware sensing-quality-based budget feasible incentive mechanism for crowdsourcing fingerprint collection. *IEEE Access*, 8:49775–49784, 2020. doi: 10.1109/ACCESS.2020.2974909.

X. Li, Q. Zhu, and X. Wang. Privacy-aware crowdsourced spectrum sensing and multi-user sharing mechanism in dynamic spectrum access networks. *IEEE Access*, 7:32971–32988, 2019. doi: 10.1109/ACCESS.2019.2901200.

Q. Ma, L. Gao, Y. Liu, and J. Huang. Incentivizing wi-fi network crowdsourcing: A contract theoretic approach. *IEEE/ACM Transactions on Networking*, 26(3):1035–1048, 2018. doi: 10.1109/TNET.2018.2812785.

V. Raida, P. Svoboda, M. Lerch, and M. Rupp. Crowdsensed performance benchmarking of mobile networks. *IEEE Access*, 7:154899–154911, 2019. doi: 10.1109/ACCESS.2019.2949051.

C. Zhao, S. Yang, X. Yang, and J. A. McCann. Rapid, user-transparent, and trustworthy device pairing for d2d-enabled mobile crowdsourcing. *IEEE Transactions on Mobile Computing*, 16(7):2008–2022, 2017. doi: 10.1109/TMC.2016.2611575.

# 12

# Problems

**Problem 1** What are the two other major components of a typical mobile crowdsourcing system, besides the MCS server?

**Problem 2** In a location-based mobile crowdsourcing application (e.g., a city guide that suggests restaurants to users), what mechanism do you suggest the mobile workers to use to preserve their privacy before publishing their locations to the server?

- (a) If the Manhattan or $l_1$ norm distance metric is used, what probability distribution do you suggest for distance perturbation?
- (b) If the Euclidean or $l_2$ norm is used as a distance metric, what probability distribution do you suggest for distance perturbation?

**Problem 3** What are the three criteria for the MCS server to design the payment mechanism to mobile workers?

**Problem 4** A task $t_j$ has the maximum value of $v_j$ for its requestor. Can you relate $v_j$ to the publishing radius of $t_j$ and the maximum privacy budget $\epsilon_{\max}$? Assume that the cost is linearly proportional to the travelling distance by a factor $\alpha$ and to the privacy budget by a factor $\beta$.

**Problem 5** Referring to how differential privacy was defined, what values of $\epsilon$ cause more privacy leakage? Larger or smaller?

**Problem 6** Using the definition of differential privacy, verify that if $\mathcal{D}_1(x, x') \leq \mathcal{D}_2(x, x')$, then $\epsilon\mathcal{D}_1(x, x')$-privacy implies $\epsilon\mathcal{D}_2(x, x')$-privacy.

**Problem 7** Formalize an integer linear programming to minimize the total travel distance in a location-based mobile crowdsourcing application. $x(w_i, t_j) = 1$ means that task $t_j$ has been allocated to worker $w_i$, while $x(w_i, t_j) = 0$ means that task $t_j$ has not been allocated to worker $w_i$.

Each mobile worker can be assigned to at most two tasks and each task needs to be assigned to four workers.

**Problem 8** Consider a location-based task for a city guide MCS platform, which involves taking up-to-date images from Airbnb homes available for short-term rental. Ivy and Mina applied for the task and used Laplace mechanism for privacy.

(a) Find the probability that the server allocates this task to Mina in terms of $f(\gamma_i, \gamma_m)$.

Note: $\gamma_i$ and $\gamma_m$ are independent noise variables related to mobile phones of Ivy and Mina, respectively.

(b) What is the above probability if the privacy budget of Ivy is 1.5 and the privacy budget of Mina is 2?

**Problem 9** Consider an attack on GPS-based vehicular mobile crowdsourcing applications in which an attacker uses end-to-end mobile emulator software to launch sybil attack to create fake traffic hotspots to re-route the cars.

- (a) How can the attacker convince the server that there is heavy traffic on a road?
- (b) Explain a graph-based defense method. How is the graph formed?
- (c) Once the graph is formed, what is the method to identify sybil nodes from real physical mobile devices?

**Problem 10** Consider the following typical energy consumption data on a mobile device:

- each hash calculation taking 0.01 ms and consuming $8.17 \times 10^{-6}$ J of energy;
- LTE upload consuming $1 \times 10^{-5}$ J/bit;
- Bluetooth consuming $2 \times 10^{-7}$ J per bit.

How much energy does the secure crowdsensed object search (discussed in Chapter 2) consume to find your lost object with the following parameters?

- Total number of mobile devices involved in the search are 1000.
- Probability that each mobile device transmits dummy tags is 80%.
- Total number of slots per frame is 400.
- 20 hash functions are used.
- Average total rounds that it takes to find the lost object is 5.

**Problem 11** In the crowdsensed object search in Chapter 2, if the output of every $h(.)$ mod $f$, where $h(.)$ is a hash function, is a discrete uniformly distributed random variable in $\{0, 1, \ldots, f - 1\}$, find the probability that no dummy tag time slot coincides with the particular time slot of the lost object. Use the parameters given in the previous question.

**Problem 12** (Chapter 2) If the transmission range of the lost object's tag is 8 m and there are totally 1000 mobile users in 100 m$^2$, what is the probability of the correct performance for the crowdsensed object search?

**Problem 13** Find the average distinct time slots for a lost object if the probability of $l$ distinct slots for the lost object is

$$\binom{f}{l}\left(\frac{1}{f}\right)^l. \tag{12.1}$$

Here, $f$ is the total number of slots in a frame, and $K$ is the total number of hash functions.

**Problem 14** Find the average number of total rounds that it takes for crowdsensed object search to terminate. Consider the following parameters in your calculations:

- $10,000$ total mobile detectors;
- each round, 40% of them are excluded from the search by the object owner;
- only one mobile detector remains in the final round.

---

Probability distributions:

Gaussian

$$f(x) = \frac{1}{\sqrt{2\pi\sigma^2}} \exp\left(\frac{-(x-\mu)^2}{2\sigma^2}\right)$$

Poisson

$$P[X = k] = \exp(-\lambda)\frac{\lambda^k}{k!}$$

Laplace

$$f(x) = \frac{\epsilon}{2} \exp(-\epsilon|x|)$$

# Index

# About the Author

**Shabnam Sodagari** received her Ph.D. from the Pennsylvania State University in electrical engineering and is a faculty member of computer engineering and computer science.